WHOLE EARTH COOK BOOK

Recipes tested in the Whole Earth Restaurant
on the University of California Campus, Santa Cruz, California

Whole Earth Cook Book

SHARON CADWALLADER · JUDI OHR

PREFACE BY PAUL LEE   ILLUSTRATED BY ANITA WALKER SCOTT

Published in association with SAN FRANCISCO BOOK COMPANY

HOUGHTON MIFFLIN COMPANY BOSTON

c 10 9 8 7 6 5

A portion of this book has appeared in *McCall's* magazine

Copyright © 1972 by San Francisco Book Company, Inc.

ISBN: 0-395-13642-3   Hardbound c
ISBN: 0-395-13748-9   Paperbound b

Library of Congress Catalog Card No.: 77-183629
Printed in the United States of America

Although the Whole Earth Restaurant is located on the campus of the
University of California in Santa Cruz, it is a private, nonprofit organi-
zation and in no way is *Whole Earth Cook Book* an official publication
of the University of California .

THIS BOOK IS DEDICATED TO A HEALTHY, HAPPY WHOLE EARTH

With love and gratitude to
the Whole Earth Restaurant family: Jane, Linda, Rock,
Cathy, Tom, Nick, Carol, Bonnie, Gene, Karen,
Paul, Ed, Herb, Jerry, Charlene, Bill,
Bob, and Jay, and the Staff of Life Bakery;
and special thanks to Jeanne for her help in editing,
typing, and assembling.

Preface

When Stuart Brand first told me about the significance of the first photograph, from outer space, of the whole earth, I didn't understand him. But I pondered it in my heart. When Stuart and Lois came through northern Wisconsin and stopped at Cisco Point, on their first Whole Earth Truck Tour, I had a little better idea of what was going down. I bought a tipi. Now that the *Whole Earth Catalog* has come and gone the message is clear.

The Whole Earth came into perspective with the photograph of the whole earth. Now every point is equidistant from every other point, as every person is equidistant from every other person. The coincidence of opposites, prophesied by that wonderful old Christian, Nicolaus Cusanus, has become a reality. The responsibility for nurturing and transforming the Whole Earth is up to us;

we are in it together to get it together, to realize in our-
selves, with one another, the Whole Earth.

There are two pieces of earth where this effort is taking
place, both of them at the University of California, Santa
Cruz. One is on a slope at the upper entrance of the University — the Student Garden Project. Dedicated to the
memories of Von Moltke and Bonhoeffer, the Garden is
the transition from the holocaust to the Whole Earth.
Dedicated to biodynamic, organic, vitalist, ecological
horticulture, the Garden, under the mastership of Alan
Chadwick, is a model of that community of wholeness
and wholesomeness the vision of the Whole Earth means
to nurture and foster.

Whole
(1) Possessing, or being in, a state of health and sound-
ness; well; sound; hence, healed.
(2) Not broken; unimpaired; integral, as in integrated,
self-integration.
(3) Containing the total amount, number; complete; entire; intact; perfect.

On another slope, as an outgrowth of the Student Garden,
the Whole Earth Restaurant is dedicated to the new sensi-
bility of the Whole Earth and the restoration of kinship
with the Whole Earth. Situated midway between the
Wilderness and the Garden, the Whole Earth Restaurant
takes part in that exodus from institutional bondage we
are all called upon to enact; this *Whole Earth Cook Book*
provides you with the recipes for doing it yourself as one
of us.
                                               Paul Lee

July 21, 1971
Cisco Point
Phelps, Wisconsin

Contents

Introduction

What are natural foods?

For many years nutritionists have been lecturing about the deficiencies in our national diet, but their audience has been very small and little of this information ever filtered through to the large middle segment of our population. However, in the last two or three years, more and more people have become aware of the need for change in their nutritional patterns. Many of the younger generation have taken the responsibility of altering their diets and are converting to pure foods with the zeal of atonement. Numerous articles have been published in national magazines and urban newspapers about the overrefinement of grain products, excessive consumption of sugar and saturated fats, and the amount of chemical additives in prepared foods. Public controversy over the indiscriminate use of pesticides and chemical fertilizers in farming initiated research in the dangers of these chemicals to human life. The results were alarming and our government has begun to abolish the use of some of the more lethal sprays.

What do all the changes signify?

Let us start at the beginning. It is a basic biological fact that no plant can be superior to the soil in which it was grown. If, after each growing season, the unused vegetation is removed from the ground that nourished it, rather than retained to decompose naturally to feed the next crop, all the important vitamins and minerals will soon disappear from the soil. This is what is happening to our large commercial farming areas. In order to increase the growing periods, each crop is being fed with chemical stimulants and fertilizers, yet each year tons of unused produce are discarded or dumped in the ocean to maintain high consumer prices. The economics are inefficient and our health is in jeopardy.

Unfortunately, there are other areas of gross negligence in our food raising. The modern feedlot techniques of the large meat producers are so unhealthy that one cattleman commented to us, "I raise a private stock for my own use." But, until the consumer demands natural raising of meat and insists that the government forbid the injecting of chemicals and ban the use of poisons and waste in animal feed, these practices will continue. At the present time the most you can do for your diet is to select the best cuts from a clean butcher shop. Avoid packaged-meat counters and do not buy prepared luncheon meats because of the questionable ingredients and chemical additives. Learn to cook glandular meats, such as liver, kidney, and sweetbreads, and the less common muscle sections, like tongue and heart. These parts of the animal are the richest in B vitamins and are cheaper than the standard cuts. Also, in some areas of the country, you can buy naturally fed meats which are not injected with chemicals. We suggest you inquire about the availability of organic meats in your area.

Chicken farmers are also guilty of malpractice in the mass production of chickens for consumption. In fact, last year California passed a law forbidding the injection of chickens with antibiotics, so gross were the results of this practice. Chickens raised on natural feeds and allowed the freedom to scratch taste much better than those who spend their lives with thousands of other chickens jammed in a building and fed nothing short of trash. Laying hens that are raised under these conditions, and without a rooster, produce eggs lacking in important hormones, enzymes, and protein found in fertilized eggs.

Along with these concerns is the condition of the fresh-water fish in the United States. So much industrial waste is dumped into our rivers and lakes that there are places where no fish is safe to be eaten. Even salt water in some of the coastal areas is so polluted that the fish are toxic. Today it is wisest to buy bottom and deep-sea fish.

Another major source of nutrition which needs improvement is the dairy industry. Not quite as careless in its practices, there is still the question of preservatives added to milk and milk products. At the same time, the pasteurization process causes a reduction in the amount of calcium and the destruction of hormones and enzymes. Raw milk and raw milk products are the best sources of these nutrients, providing — and this is important — the milk comes from a clean, certified herd and is handled very carefully. There are few of these herds in the country, so you will probably have to continue using pasteurized milk for now. Try to find a local dairy, though, and check out their practices.

There have already been many articles published about the enormous intake of sugar in the United States. A few of our recipes call for natural sugar, but we think natural sugars are mainly a psychological comfort — they look natural. We urge substitution of uncooked, unfiltered honeys for sugar whenever possible. We also recommend the use of sea salt to avoid the chemicals in ordinary table salt.

Natural foods, then, are simply those vegetables, fruits, and grains which are grown in soils rich in organic matter, without chemical treatment, and animals that are raised on natural feeds and allowed to move freely in healthy pastures. It is not the basic ingredients of the American diet which are in question, but the quality of these ingredients which invites criticism. We do not need a larger variety of foodstuffs, more attractive packaging, larger economy sizes, pretty, symmetrical produce. We need nutritional quality. If we are made aware of the total cycle of the food we eat, we will become more conscious of its quality.

We urge you to pressure local farmers to return to organic gardening methods, to demand that natural products be stocked on supermarket shelves, and that harmful and nutritionless foods be removed. For many years the so-called health food store held a mystique alien to most Americans. Now, all over the country, natural food stores are springing up full of products we will be discussing in this book. More natural grains and flours are appearing in the big supermarkets. We are very optimistic.*

*A complete list of organic food sources in the United States can be found in the Notes (see page 111).

We hope the following recipes will stimulate your interest in planning a healthful diet. Do not discard your favorite recipes; instead, substitute natural ingredients and prepare your foods carefully to guard against the loss of nutrients. None of our recipes are complicated, as we want to turn you on to the relaxation in simple, natural cooking. The country kitchen is a traditional gathering place. Let this style pull you into the fun of cooking. We at the Whole Earth Restaurant make a party out of preparing meals. We hope you will do the same with your family and friends, and that every day brings another party.

WHOLE EARTH COOK BOOK

Soups

A French friend once lamented, "How will my poor child ever adjust to these canned soups in the United States?" To Americans a fine soup is identified with an exceptionally fine cook, but to the French making good soup is assumed. In actuality there are only a few tricks and, with a little knowledge and a minimum of effort, you can prepare a delicious soup every time.

One secret is the stock. In all your food preparations keep the soup stock in a corner of your kitchen thoughts. Vegetable cooking water should be saved and refrigerated. If you have access to fresh organic vegetables, save parings, scraps, pits, seeds, outer lettuce leaves and fertile-egg shells. (Commercial eggs are often sprayed with disinfectants.) Put them in a bag or container in the refrigerator until you have enough to make a good stock, about 1 or 2 pounds. Dump them in a large pot with 1 or 2 quarts of water and simmer, covered, for 30 to 45 minutes. Strain and store stock in refrigerator.

Learn to recycle scraps into the next soup. All leftovers — meat, vegetables, salads, grains, eggs, cheese, even bread — can be added to soup. We are including a recipe for making meat stock which can be frozen or refrigerated for later use (see below). When you are growing sprouts (see page 18) be sure to save the sprout water for stock. You can make wonderful soups very quickly if you have a good, hearty stock.

When preparing soup, add the vegetables in the last stage so the vitamins and minerals do not evaporate in cooking. If you are using a vegetable stock without meat, it is best to sauté some of the vegetables before adding them to the stock. This helps to hold the flavor in the vegetable, and the oil or butter adds richness to the soup. We have found that a flavorful addition to a stock needing a tomato touch is to add V-8 juice rather than tomato juice, along with fresh tomatoes if you wish.

A hearty soup served with whole-grain bread and a vegetable salad is a very satisfying meal.

Meat Soup Stock

Some butcher shops give marrow bones and chicken feet away. Soup bones are always very cheap. Use young beef or veal bones, ribs, back, shoulder, or any marrow bone will make good jelly stock. Oxtail, shank, and short rib cost more but have good flavor for minestrone. Use chicken feet or backs if available.

Simmer bones together with 1 to 2 quarts water, depending on the amount of bones, and ¼ cup vinegar,

2 bay leaves, salt and pepper. Simmer, covered, about 3 hours. Remove any meat and discard bones. Chill stock and skim off any excess fat. Freeze if desired.

Cheese Soybean Soup

Follow directions for cooking soybeans in Basic Soybean Recipe (see page 36).

Mash soybeans with 1 large can of V-8 juice. You can use a blender. Place them in a soup pot.

Sauté and add to soup:

3 tablespoons oil	2 stalks chopped celery, both
1 small onion, chopped	stalks and leaves
1 clove garlic, mashed	

Add:

1½ cups grated cheese, Cheddar or Jack

Simmer for 30 minutes and season to taste. Serves 5 to 6.

Onion Soup

¼ cup butter or margarine	1½ cups rich beef broth
3 large onions, sliced	2½ cups water
3 tablespoons flour	½ cup grated Parmesan cheese
1½ cups rich chicken broth	

Heat butter and sauté onions until golden and tender. Sprinkle with flour. Gradually stir in chicken and beef broth and water. Simmer, stirring occasionally, for 15 minutes or until onions are tender. Sprinkle with cheese. Salt may be added. Serves 5 to 6.

Easy Oyster or Clam Chowder

2 pieces bacon, chopped	1 (10-ounce) can oysters or
1 small onion, chopped	clams
2 stalks celery, chopped	salt and pepper
1 quart water	½ teaspoon each of dried thyme,
3 potatoes, cut up	tarragon, and oregano
3 carrots, cut up	1 cup canned milk

Cook bacon halfway; then add onion and celery and sauté together. Meanwhile, put water in soup pot and simmer potatoes and carrots. When nearly tender add oysters or clams (include liquid), salt, pepper, thyme, tarragon, and oregano. Simmer 10 minutes. Add the sautéed bacon and vegetables. Just before serving (off fire), add milk. Heat through without boiling. Serves 4 to 5 depending on appetite.

VARIATION: For Manhattan style add 1 (12-ounce) can V-8 juice together with clams or oysters. Caraway seeds may be added.

Split Pea Soup with Ham Hock

½ ham hock	1 small onion, chopped
¼ teaspoon dried savory	salt and pepper
1 clove garlic, mashed	

Follow directions for Split Pea–Vegetable Stew (see page 40); however, after peas have cooked 1 hour add the ingredients above.

Simmer, covered, for 1½ to 2 more hours. Add more water if too thick. Caraway seeds may be added before serving. Serves 5 to 6.

Vegetable Minestrone

2 quarts vegetable cooking
water
½ cup barley
1 large onion, sliced
½ cup chopped fresh parsley
2 cloves garlic, mashed
3 tablespoons oil
1 (14½-ounce) can tomatoes
1 (12-ounce) can V-8 juice
2 cups lima beans, cooked and
mashed

1 (15-ounce) can kidney beans
and liquid, or cooked
equivalent
3 or 4 carrots, sliced thin
1 stalk celery, chopped
½ teaspoon dried oregano
1 bay leaf
salt and pepper
3 tablespoons red wine

Bring water to a boil; add barley and simmer until tender, 45 minutes to 1 hour. Meanwhile sauté onion, parsley, and garlic in oil. Mix all ingredients in soup pot and simmer, covered, for 1 to 1½ hours. Before serving add 3 tablespoons red wine. Serve with grated Parmesan. Serves 6 to 8.

OPTIONAL ADDITION: cooked whole-wheat or soy macaroni may be added in last half-hour.

Spanish Gazpacho

4 cups chicken broth, chilled
2 tablespoons olive oil
⅓ cup lime juice
3 or 4 tomatoes, diced

1 red onion, diced
2 large green peppers, diced
1 stalk celery, diced
dash of Tabasco sauce

Mix all the ingredients together. Vegetables must be diced fine. Add Tabasco sauce to taste. Chill thoroughly before serving. Serves 6.

Spinach Soup

4 cups salted water	2 tablespoons oil
2 bunches spinach, chopped	½ cup thinly sliced onions

Bring water to a boil, add spinach, and simmer for 5 to 7 minutes. Meanwhile, in the oil, sauté onions until they are clear. Add them to the spinach together with:

½ cup evaporated milk	1 cup cooked rice, barley,
1 teaspoon curry powder, or	potatoes, or any leftover grain
to taste	

Salt to taste and heat thoroughly. Serve with lemon wedges. Serves 4 to 6.

Green Soup

Simmer for 20 minutes in 1½ cups water:

½ cup diced green pepper	¼ cup chopped onion
2 cups chopped broccoli	

Next, mix these vegetables well in the blender until they are puréed. Place in a soup pot and add:

1 tablespoon butter	½ cup buttermilk
1 cup evaporated milk	½ teaspoon curry powder
salt to taste	

Heat through and serve. This is also delicious served cold with lemon. Serves 4.

Cabbage-Potato Borscht

In a large soup pot, cook until tender with salt and pepper in 1 quart vegetable cooking water:

1 medium onion, sliced   1 small cabbage, shredded

Meanwhile, in another pot, cook in 1 quart vegetable cooking water:

3 or 4 potatoes, diced   4 or 5 carrots, diced

When fork tender, drain potato water into cabbage broth. Mash potatoes and carrots together with:

½ pint sour cream   1 teaspoon dried dill weed (optional)

Next, add the sour-cream mixture to the broth, very slowly to avoid curdling. Stir continually during this part. Add more salt and pepper to taste. Serve immediately.

Pumpkin-Mushroom Soup

½ pound mushrooms, sliced   1 (1-pound) can pumpkin
½ cup chopped onion   1 tablespoon honey
2 tablespoons butter or oil   dash of nutmeg
2 tablespoons flour   salt and pepper
1 tablespoon curry powder   1 cup evaporated milk
3 cups chicken broth

Sauté mushrooms and onion in butter or oil. Add flour and curry and stir. Gradually add broth. Add everything but the milk and cook, stirring, for 10 to 15 minutes. Add milk and heat through without boiling. May top with sour cream or yogurt (see page 40). Serves 6.

Fresh Cream of Tomato Soup

2 quarts water or vegetable
  cooking water
3 or 4 bouillon cubes,
  vegetable or chicken
1 large onion, chopped
10 to 12 medium tomatoes,
  peeled and chopped
2 cups chopped celery

1 teaspoon salt
3 or 4 tablespoons honey
2 tablespoons butter
1 teaspoon paprika
2 cups evaporated milk, or 1 cup
  homogenized milk and 1 cup
  light cream

Bring water to boil. Add bouillon cubes, vegetables, and salt. Simmer 30 minutes. Transfer to blender and mix well. Add honey, butter, and paprika. Return to pan and add milk slowly to prevent curdling. Heat through and serve. Serves 6 to 8.

Navy Bean Soup

Cook 2 cups navy beans according to the Basic Bean Recipe (see page 35). Meanwhile, in ½ cup of olive oil, sauté:

2 large onions, sliced
2 garlic cloves, crushed

1 cup fresh, chopped parsley

Combine this with the beans and add:

½ teaspoon dried thyme
¼ cup tomato paste
juice of ½ lemon

2 tablespoons salt
pepper

Simmer for 30 minutes. Serves 8.

Salads and Vegetables

SALADS   In this era of organicity, of vegetarian diets and home gardening, we find an increasing interest in the preparation of fresh and cooked vegetables. Included in this section are a few hints to help give more nutrition and enjoyment to this part of your diet. Given the vast selection of fresh vegetables on the market today, the traditional head-lettuce-and-tomato salad and cabbage slaw are relatively unimaginative. Also, the variety of vegetables being frozen each year increases and, in certain areas during the winter season, when fresh vegetables are not easily obtainable, you can defrost some of these vegetables and use them in fresh salads.

In preparing salads, we urge you to use as many raw vegetables and fruits as are available in your area. Use a vegetable brush and scrub root vegetables. Wash green, leafy vegetables quickly and dry them well. Do not soak vegetables, because many nutrients will be released into the water. When trying new vegetables in a salad, grate them or slice them very thin. When using greens new to you, chop fine and use the young leaves. Combine fruits and vegetables together. Experiment and find your favorites. Along with lettuce, tomatoes, avocados, onions, and cucumbers, you can use:

parsley
kale
endive
turnip tops
spinach
New Zealand spinach
cabbages (Chinese, Savoy)
escarole
beet tops
Swiss chard
collard greens
dandelion greens (slightly bitter)

broccoli and cauliflower leaves
raw cauliflower and broccoli
young nasturtium leaves
young peas with pod
young milkweed leaves (grow wild)
any root vegetables (beets, turnips, parsnips, rutabagas, etc.)
alfalfa or mung-bean sprouts

Fresh sprouts are a superb source of vitamins, five times higher than the seed-grain form. Any seed, whole grain, dried pea, or dried bean, can be sprouted. Alfalfa and mung bean are the most frequently sold. (See page 18 for instructions for Sprouting Seeds.)

Additional suggestions:

grated cheese
grated hard-boiled eggs
chopped nuts

sunflower, pumpkin, poppy, or sesame seeds

We include a recipe for a basic dressing, a yogurt dressing, and a delicious mayonnaise from which you can make your own favorite cream dressings.

VEGETABLES   There are two important rules for cooking vegetables: (1) wash well, but do not soak, and (2) do not overcook. If anything, vegetables should be undercooked. They should be firm, and the stems of green leafy vegetables should be slightly crisp. Americans are still learning to cook vegetables tastily and nutritiously. The easiest way to avoid overcooking vegetables is to purchase a vegetable steamer. We recommend the stainless-steel variety which is collapsible and fits any pot. Besides losing fewer nutrients in the water, you will find the taste fresher and better. The water you use under the steamer should be retained and refrigerated for use in soups or cooking grains. It is nice to add a little oil, garlic, and herbs while steaming. Salt just before serving. Another good way to prepare vegetables is in an Oriental manner. Chop the vegetables into equal-sized pieces. Sauté the vegetables in a heavy skillet in a little oil. Reduce the heat to the lowest point, cover, and steam briefly.

Herbs and garlic on vegetables will turn your taste around. Vegetables are the best reason for raising herbs. Even if you live in the city, you can plant herbs in flowerpots or in the center of cement blocks. If you do not have access to fresh herbs, the dried variety can be substituted as long as you remember to use one half the amount required for fresh herbs.

Spinach Salad

2 bunches freshly picked
  spinach
½ onion, sliced
2 hard-boiled eggs, diced
2 tablespoons vegetable oil

4 tablespoons wine vinegar
4 tablespoons water
1 teaspoon salt
½ teaspoon pepper

Clean spinach carefully, as each leaf can hold dirt. Place clean, washed leaves in a bowl and add the onion and eggs. Mix together oil, vinegar, water, salt, and pepper. Pour over the salad and toss lightly.

Super Caesar Salad

2 tablespoons salad oil
1 garlic clove, minced
2 cups bread cubes
1 large head romaine lettuce
1 large head iceberg lettuce
¼ cup grated Parmesan
  cheese

¼ cup crumbled blue cheese
½ cup salad oil
¼ cup lemon juice
¼ teaspoon Tabasco sauce
¾ teaspoon salt
¼ teaspoon dry mustard
1 egg

Heat the salad oil and garlic in a skillet. Add the bread cubes and sauté until lightly browned. Remove and set aside. Tear crisp, chilled lettuce into bite-sized pieces and place in a salad bowl. Sprinkle with Parmesan and blue cheese. Combine salad oil, lemon juice, Tabasco sauce, salt, and dry mustard and shake to blend. Pour over the salad greens and toss lightly. Then break the raw egg into salad greens and toss lightly until the egg particles disappear. Add the croutons and again toss lightly. Serves 6.

Lemon Bean Salad

2 cups dried white beans
¼ cup lemon juice
½ teaspoon pepper
¼ cup chopped chives

½ cup olive oil
2 cloves garlic, minced
1 cup shredded lettuce

Cook beans as directed in the Basic Bean Recipe (see page 35). Mix together all the remaining ingredients. Beat well and pour over the beans. Chill thoroughly.

Special Summer Salad

1 pineapple
6 apricots, cut up
1 banana, sliced
½ cantaloupe, or other
    melon, diced

1 cup grapes
1 cup shredded coconut
    (preferably unsweetened)
1 pint sour cream
¼ cup chopped walnuts

Chill pineapple overnight. Slice in half. Cut out core and then cut out pineapple. Put in bowl along with other cut-up fruit. Add coconut, sour cream, and nuts. Mix well. Chill until ready to serve.

Cheese Zucchini Salad

2 hard-boiled eggs, grated
2 medium zucchini, grated
1 cup shredded lettuce
garlic salt

1 small onion, thinly sliced
1 cup grated cheese
salt, pepper, and dill weed
Basic Dressing (see page 19)

Combine all ingredients, adding salt, pepper, dill weed, garlic salt, and Basic Dressing to taste. Toss lightly.

Caraway Cabbage Salad

½ medium-sized red cabbage
½ medium-sized green
  cabbage
½ medium onion

Basic Dressing (see page 19)
salt, pepper, and garlic salt
1 teaspoon caraway seeds

Shred and chop cabbage as thin as possible. Slice onion and then pull it apart. Toss with Basic Dressing, salt, pepper, and garlic salt, adding as much of these as desired to satisfy your taste. Add caraway seeds and toss lightly.

Sprouting Seeds

Use approximately 2 tablespoons of seeds, or about 4 tablespoons of legumes. Put your seeds in a quart jar. Cover them with warm water and soak for 8 hours. Drain off the liquid through a cheesecloth or wire mesh which has been placed under the ring of the jar lid. Rinse the seeds and drain them well. Now lay the jar on its side. Rinse the sprouts two or three times a day and place the jar back on its side. Be careful not to let the sprouts set too long in water or dry out, as this will cause the crop to spoil. Within three or four days the sprouts will have developed completely and they will be ready to eat and/or refrigerate.

It is advisable to keep sprout jar in a dark place (the cupboard) for the first two or three days and bring it out in the light on the last day when the chlorophyll develops. This process generally produces nice, green sprouts.

Legumes and seeds for sprouting can be obtained in natural food stores and mills. We particularly recommend using alfalfa seeds because of their delicate taste.

Apple-Raisin Slaw

1 cup seedless raisins
¼ cup rosé wine
1 tablespoon lemon juice

3 apples, diced without paring
4 cups raw cabbage, shredded
1 cup mayonnaise (see page 20)

Combine raisins with wine. Cover and let stand several hours or overnight. Sprinkle lemon juice over coarsely diced apples and stir well. Mix with raisins and wine and shredded cabbage. Add the mayonnaise and season to taste. Toss and serve at once. This goes well with ham, roast pork, or turkey. Serves 6 to 8.

Basic Dressing

For a large salad to serve 6 to 8.

3 tablespoons oil
salt, pepper, garlic salt
3 tablespoons lemon juice or
wine vinegar

herbs and seeds (select from oregano, basil, tarragon, thyme, curry powder, caraway, dill, or sesame seeds)

1. Be sure that the vegetables are free from water.
2. Sprinkle oil on salad and toss well to coat all the vegetables. Oil holds in the nutrients.
3. Add salt, pepper, garlic salt, herbs and/or seeds, and toss again.
4. Sprinkle in lemon juice or vinegar, toss well, and serve immediately. A dash of soy sauce is nice with lemon dressing.

If this dressing is too tart, decrease the amount of vinegar or lemon. Experiment and find your own taste. Once you get the knack of this method of dressing salads, you will look forward to preparing salads daily.

Mayonnaise

Blend in a blender:

2 egg yolks
½ teaspoon salt
2 tablespoons white-wine
  vinegar

2 tablespoons lemon juice
¼ teaspoon dry mustard
dash of cayenne

Next, slowly blend in up to 2 cups oil, depending on desired thickness. The more oil, the thicker the mayonnaise will be.

Yogurt-Olive Dressing

1 cup yogurt (see page 40)
½ cup mayonnaise (see above)
1 (4½-ounce) can chopped
  olives

salt, pepper, garlic powder
dash of Tabasco sauce

Mix all the ingredients well. This dressing is best on heavy vegetables such as cabbage, beets, carrots, etc.

Vegetable Loaf

1 medium eggplant
1 cup diced celery
1 medium onion, chopped
1 tomato, diced
4 tablespoons butter
1 egg
½ cup bread crumbs

½ teaspoon dried oregano
1 tablespoon wheat germ
1 tablespoon tofu (see page 34)
garlic powder
salt
⅓ cup bread crumbs

Peel and chop eggplant fine, or grind it in a meat or food

grinder. Place in a frying pan, add vegetables, and sauté in butter. Remove to a mixing bowl and let cool. Add egg, bread crumbs, oregano, wheat germ, tofu, garlic, and salt to taste, and place in greased baking dish. Sprinkle with remaining bread crumbs and bake in 350° preheated oven for 25 minutes.

Greens or Green Beans with Bacon

2 bunches greens, or	1 clove garlic, mashed
1½ pounds green beans	1 medium onion, sliced
2 slices of bacon, diced	salt and pepper

Wash and chop greens, or trim beans. In heavy skillet, brown bacon until almost crisp. Add mashed garlic, greens or beans, and onion, and sauté lightly. Beans may be steamed slightly first. Cover and reduce heat; steam, turning occasionally until the leaves of the greens are limp and/or the beans are only slightly crisp. Add salt and pepper to taste.

Eggplant Pizza

1 medium eggplant, unpeeled and sliced thin	2 cloves garlic, mashed
1 can pizza sauce (about 1⅓ cups)	1 teaspoon dried oregano
	2 cups grated Jack or mozzarella cheese
1 cup chopped green onions	1 small can sliced black olives

Place eggplant slices in a shallow baking dish. Mix sauce, onions, garlic, and oregano, and pour equally over eggplant slices. Top with cheese and olives. Bake at 350° for 20 minutes. Eat with a fork. Serves 4 to 6.

Mexican Stuffed Zucchini

This is for a large squash. Simply scale down recipe for smaller ones.

1 large, 3- to 5-pound squash
2 cans enchilada sauce
1 cup water
2 slices bacon, chopped
½ cup chopped bell pepper
1 onion, chopped
2 cups chopped mushrooms
2 cloves garlic, mashed
1 cup cooked sweet corn

½ cup sliced black olives
3 cups cooked rice
1 can chili salsa or
   Mexican sauce
2 eggs, beaten
salt and pepper
1 cup grated dry Parmesan or
   Romano cheese

Slice the squash lengthwise and scoop the center out, leaving a shell one half-inch thick. If the center is very pithy, discard. If it is firm, it can be chopped and combined with the stuffing.

Pour the two cans of enchilada sauce combined with the water in a large, shallow pan. Place both halves of the squash, skin side down, in the pan, and steam, covered with foil, at 325° for 30 minutes. Sauté the bacon for 4 to 5 minutes. Then add the bell pepper, onion, mushrooms, and garlic and cook until onion is clear. Remove. Add corn, olives, rice, chili salsa or other Mexican sauce, beaten eggs, and salt and pepper, and mix all together.

Scoop mixture into the squash shells; top with the dry, grated cheese. Cover again with foil and bake until squash shell is tender, to taste, approximately 30 to 45 minutes. Serves 8.

Squash with Mushrooms

6 summer, crookneck, or
   zucchini squashes
½ teaspoon salt
⅛ teaspoon pepper
1 tablespoon butter or
   margarine

1 large onion, chopped
½ cup Zinfandel or other red
   table wine
1 (8-ounce) can tomato sauce
¼ pound fresh mushrooms,
   washed and cut up

Wash squash and cut into cubes. In large saucepan, combine squash with all remaining ingredients. Simmer slowly until squash is just tender (5 to 7 minutes). This is a hearty dish, a good accompaniment to white fish or beef. Serves 3 to 4.

Baked Asparagus Almond

2 pounds fresh asparagus
2 cups white sauce
lemon

dash of Worcestershire sauce
¼ pound sharp cheese, grated
1 cup blanched almonds

Cook asparagus until just tender. Do not overcook. Make a white sauce and season it with lemon and a dash of Worcestershire sauce. In a greased casserole arrange alternate layers of asparagus and white sauce to which one half of the grated cheese has been added. Finish with sprinkle of cheese and the almonds. Brown lightly in the oven. Serves 5 to 6. (Canned asparagus may be substituted for cooked, fresh asparagus.)

Kale Sauté

1 large bunch kale	2 tablespoons oil
1 large onion, sliced thin	3 teaspoons prepared mustard
1 clove garlic, mashed	

Pull kale off the stalk and chop coarsely, saving the stalks for stock. Steam until tender, about 30 minutes. Meanwhile sauté onion and garlic in oil. Add kale to onion and stir in mustard. Serves 4 to 6.

Mushrooms may be added with the onion.

Red Cabbage (Sweet and Sour)

1 large head red cabbage	½ teaspoon cinnamon
1 tablespoon vegetable oil	1 tablespoon salt
6 whole cloves	½ teaspoon pepper
⅓ cup honey or ½ cup	2 apples, shredded
natural sugar	2 onions, shredded
2 cups red vinegar	

Chop the red cabbage, or shred in blender. Place in large pot together with the remaining ingredients. Simmer for approximately 5 hours.

Chived Carrots

5 or 6 medium-sized carrots	⅛ teaspoon pepper
¼ cup butter or margarine	1 tablespoon snipped chives
¼ teaspoon salt	

Scrub and chop carrots and cook until slightly tender. Melt butter or margarine in skillet. Add carrots, salt, pepper, and snipped chives. Heat until hot and coat with butter. Serves 6.

Sandwiches

Americans could learn from the Scandinavians about sandwich preparation. The lack of imagination in our lunches has broken ground for thousands of prepared-hamburger havens.

At the Whole Earth Restaurant, we have developed a style of preparing sandwiches where presumption is the first step of preparation. Try anything and everything and, in spite of a few failures, you will have a majority of delicious successes.

We use eggs, scrambled, hard-boiled, and grated; various cheeses, grated; chopped clams, tuna, or shrimp; cottage cheese, cream cheese, or mashed soybeans, in combinations or separately as a base to which we have successfully added parsley, spinach, watercress, onions, alfalfa sprouts, and mushrooms. Sometimes we sauté the vegetables; often we add them raw and chopped fine. We add something crunchy to nearly every sandwich, such as celery, bean sprouts, water chestnuts, sunflower or pumpkin seeds, and ground or chopped nuts of every variety.

Some of the popular sandwiches are: grated egg, ground almond, and green onion; tuna, red onion, and sunflower seeds; and grated cheese, sautéed mushrooms, and alfalfa sprouts. It is difficult to give measurements, as we prepare our fillings "a taste to each step."

One specialty for which we will include a recipe is our Soybean Spread. You can add to and improve upon this. Try combining it with tuna or egg or cheese.

Soybean Spread

Cook 2 cups of soybeans according to the Basic Soybean Recipe (see page 36). When tender, mash well with whatever liquid remains. (They are very hard to mash after refrigeration.) Set aside.

Sauté for 5 minutes:

> 1½ slices finely chopped bacon

Add and sauté for 5 more minutes:

1 cup finely chopped onions	1 cup fresh, finely chopped
2 cloves garlic, mashed	parsley

Mix sautéed ingredients with the soybeans along with:

1 teaspoon dried oregano	1 tablespoon soy sauce
¾ cup mayonnaise (see page 20)	salt to taste

Mix thoroughly, using more or less mayonnaise to get the desired consistency for spreading.

NOTE: Vegetarian bacon bits may be used instead of bacon. If so, then the vegetables should be sautéed in oil, and the bacon bits added last.

Nonmeat Protein Dishes

Nutritional research indicates that the need for protein increases from infancy to age twenty. After twenty the need decreases slightly, except in periods of stress or pregnancy and lactation. Lactation is the time a woman's protein need is greatest.

Briefly, nitrogen-containing amino acids are the essence of protein. These amino acids (22 in all) are vital to the formation and tone of body tissue. Many of these amino acids can be manufactured in the body cells from nitrogen released from other proteins to combine with fat or sugar. Eight cannot be produced by this process and they are referred to as essential amino acids; however, all amino acids are essential to good health. Foods containing these eight amino acids are considered complete proteins. The richest animal sources are egg yolks, milk, and organ meats, especially liver and kidney.

If one wishes to forgo the eating of animal protein, the utmost care must be given to obtaining protein from alternate foods each day. The best sources, in order of their value, are: soybeans, wheat germ, brewer's yeast, nuts and seeds, and whole grains. Other fair sources are dried beans, peas, and rice. When the diet is without meat, poultry, or fish, but dairy products are eaten occasionally, it is necessary to obtain the purest sources. Raw milk from a certified dairy or cow is excellent. If it is unavailable, pasteurized or homogenized milk should be fortified with powdered milk. Cheese from unpasteurized milk is delicious, but most any natural cheese not marked *processed* and without additives can be used safely; however, Cheddar-type cheese usually contains artificial coloring.

Another dairy product, yogurt, is known for its assistance in maintaining essential bacteria in the digestive tract. It has been a staple for many centuries in the Middle Eastern and Balkan countries. We cannot conscientiously recommend using the yogurts sold in supermarkets because of the additives and artificial flavorings. There is also a question involving the value of these cultures. On the other hand, the tasty, healthful yogurts sold in natural food stores tend to be expensive when served daily. Therefore, we include a basic recipe for making yogurt and information on buying electric incubators in the Notes (see page 111).

As mentioned in the Introduction, fertile eggs are an important addition to a good diet. It may take some scouting to find them in the large cities, but results are well worth it.

Whether to use butter or margarine is an issue for the modern American. Since most margarines contain only slightly less saturated fatty acids than butter, and vitamin A is added to margarine, the choice may be based on the ingredients and taste. Most margarines in supermarkets contain preservatives, so it is wise to read the labels. The natural food stores sell some excellent margarines without chemical additives which are made from good oils or from soybean extracts.

A description of wheat germ and rice will be found in the discussion of grains on pages 59–62.

Nuts and sunflower, sesame, and pumpkin seeds can be purchased, shelled and unshelled, in natural food stores. High in protein, vitamins, and minerals, they make excellent snacks for children and interesting cooking and baking ingredients. Uncooked nuts, in addition to providing a good source of protein, contain the three essential fatty acids. These are the fatty acids not manufactured by body sugar and are obtained only through food sources. They are also known as unsaturated fatty acids. Their important function is to combine with and transport other nutrients to various parts of the body to build cells. This vital process is inhibited by the adding of the chemical hydrogen which turns fats into solids. Vegetable oils, nuts, and unhydrogenated nut butters are the best sources of unsaturated fatty acids.

If oils are subject to the high heat of refinement, the vitamin E is lost and lecithin, a substance essential to the breakdown and absorption of fats, is discarded. When a fat or oil is left unrefrigerated or exposed to oxygen, not only is the vitamin E destroyed, but the oil or fat becomes rancid and destroys the existing vitamin E in the body. Preservatives are added to modern vegetable oils to inhibit rancidity. We suggest using cold-pressed oils which are subjected to less heat in the extraction process and are free from preservatives. We prefer safflower for an all-purpose oil. Cold-pressed corn, soy, sesame, and olive oils are also sold in natural food stores.

All dried legumes contain some protein. Split peas, lentils, and navy, lima, kidney, and pinto beans should be used, along with other protein foods. Soybeans, however, are an exception. Native to the Orient, they are relatively new to this country. They are amazingly healthful, as high in protein as meat. They are considered a complete protein, or one that contains the eight amino acids. Since they taste different from other legumes and some varieties take more cooking time, they need careful, imaginative preparation. Keep trying to find a recipe that works with your family. They are an outstanding nutritional addition.

Natural food stores carry other soybean products which should be included in a protein-conscious diet. Soy grits, for example, are soybeans broken into small pieces. They are delicious in breads, nut and meat loaves, and casseroles. They should be softened in boiling water for five to ten minutes before using. Another is tofu, or soybean curd or soy cheese. It can be found in Oriental markets, as well as in some neighborhood markets, and in natural food stores. The light, soft consistency and bland taste make it easy to use as an addition or substitute in your favorite recipes. Unfortunately, some tofu brands contain a preservative, so check this when shopping. Soy and/or wheat macaroni noodles are also available and are superior in taste to the bleached flour pasta found everywhere.

Before turning to protein recipes, we should mention nutritional powdered yeasts. Long popular with natural-food enthusiasts, they are specially valuable to people under stress or using a great deal of physical strength. Yeast is a splendid source of B vitamins and minerals. The pick-up can be felt immediately. Unfortunately, the taste is unusual and it should be introduced in small quantities. Care should be given to selecting the most palatable yeast, since there are several varieties. Try it in fruit juice first. We take it in milk. Experiment with baked goods, casseroles, and any recipe where its taste will be neutralized.

Basic Bean Recipe

Use for white, navy, kidney, pinto, lima, or other dry beans except soybeans. (See Basic Soybean Recipe, page 36.)

> 1 quart water or   2 cups beans
>   vegetable cooking water

Bring the water or vegetable cooking water to a full boil. Add beans slowly so that the boiling does not stop. Cover and reduce to simmer. Cook until nearly tender, about 2 hours, before adding salt or any other ingredient.

California Quiche

> 1 pound summer, zucchini,   1½ to 2 cups grated cheese —
>   yellow (or mixed) squash,   Swiss desired, any will do
>   or chopped Swiss chard, or   salt and pepper to taste
>   mixed squash and greens   ½ teaspoon each of dried
> ½ onion, thinly sliced   oregano and basil
> 4 eggs

Steam squash and onion. Do not oversteam. Meanwhile beat the eggs and add the grated cheese. Mash squash, don't purée as chunks are good, and add to eggs. Add salt, pepper, oregano, and basil. Pour into greased baking dish and bake covered in 325° oven until set, about 30 to 40 minutes.

Perfect as second dish at dinner.

VARIATION: For a one-dish meal, add fresh crab, shrimp, or any leftover cut-up fowl.

Nut Loaf

1 large bunch of greens (chard, spinach, turnip, or beet)	1 teaspoon dried oregano
	2 cups ground almonds, walnuts, or pecans, or in combination
¼ cup oil	1 cup dried whole-wheat bread crumbs
1 medium onion, sliced thin and chopped	½ cup wheat germ
2 tablespoons fresh, chopped parsley	½ cup catsup
1 garlic clove, mashed	1 tablespoon soy sauce

Chop and steam greens for 5 minutes. Sauté in oil the onion, parsley, garlic, and oregano. Combine all remaining ingredients. (Incidentally, ground nuts are better than chopped, which tend to become too dry.) Shape into a loaf and bake at 350° for 30 minutes. This loaf is not as firm as a meat loaf, so cut gently.

Basic Soybean Recipe

2 cups dried soybeans	2½ cups water

To prepare: Soak soybeans in 1 cup water for 1 to 2 hours; then place in flat dish in freezing compartment overnight.

To cook: Remove from freezer; crack to remove from tray and drop into 1½ cups boiling water. Cover. Reduce heat to simmer for 3 to 4 hours. The last hour is the time to add onions, seasonings, oil or ham, spices, tomatoes, or soy sauce. There are many ways to improve the palatability of soybeans. Imagination and experimentation may create a favorite recipe.

Super Soybean Casserole

1 slice salt pork or 2 or 3
slices bacon, or may sub-
stitute with 2 tablespoons
of oil, then top last few
minutes with vegetarian
bacon bits
1 green pepper, diced
1 onion, chopped

1 garlic clove, mashed
1 cup milk
2 teaspoons flour
2 teaspoons butter
2 cups cooked soybeans (see
Basic Soybean Recipe, page
36)
salt and pepper to taste

Chop salt pork or bacon and brown in frying pan. Meanwhile add vegetables to half-cooked meat and sauté together with garlic. Then make white sauce of milk, flour,
and butter. Add both mixtures to soybeans. (These should
have no excess liquid after cooking. If so, pour into freezer
jar and save for soup.) Add seasonings. Put in medium
oven dish and bake at 350°. Serves 4 to 5.

Tofu-Egg Omelet

½ pound tofu (see page 34)
8 eggs, slightly beaten
½ cup wheat germ
½ cup whole-wheat flour

2 teaspoons salt
1 teaspoon dried oregano
1 teaspoon baking powder
2 tablespoons oil

Mix all ingredients, except the oil, well. Put oil in a 9-inch,
heavy frying pan and let it get quite hot over a medium
heat. Pour in batter and reduce heat. Cook on the first
side until fairly well set. Then turn and continue to turn
occasionally until the center is firm and can be pierced
with a toothpick cleanly. This turning usually takes about
45 minutes over a low heat. Cut in pie wedges.

Simple Mexican Pinto Beans

5 cups water
2 cups pinto beans
salt
2 cloves garlic, mashed

½ medium onion, sliced
2 tablespoons vegetable oil or
½ ham hock

Bring water to a boil and add beans slowly, trying not to stifle the boil. Reduce heat and simmer for 30 minutes. Add salt, garlic, and onion. Simmer another 30 minutes. Add oil or ham hock, and cook until beans are tender. Makes a good broth. Serve in bowls with warm Whole-Wheat Tortillas (see page 84).

Cottage Cheese Lunch Loaf

1 pint large-curd cottage
  cheese
2 green onions, finely
  chopped

½ cup chopped walnuts
2 tablespoons soy sauce
dash of paprika

Mix all ingredients together and form a loaf on a flat serving dish. Chill for 3 hours. Serve on top of lettuce leaves.

Cottage Cheese Soufflé

⅓ cup oil
¾ cup flour
¾ cup milk
1 teaspoon each of salt and
  pepper

4 eggs, separated
2 cups large-curd cottage cheese
½ cup Swiss cheese, grated
1 teaspoon curry powder
juice of 1 lemon

Heat oil in 1-quart saucepan. Add flour and stir constantly while adding milk gradually. Cook until a thick sauce. Remove from heat. Add salt and pepper, well-beaten egg yolks, cottage cheese, grated cheese, curry, and lemon juice. Fold in stiffly beaten egg whites. Pour into a 1½-quart baking dish. Bake 1 hour at 300°. Serve immediately. Serves 3 to 4.

Macaroni, Egg, and Cheese

1½ quarts salted water
2 cups soy, wheat, or sesame macaroni
2 cups Jack or Cheddar-type cheese
3 eggs, well beaten with 2 tablespoons milk or cream

salt and pepper
⅓ cup whole-wheat bread crumbs
2 tablespoons wheat germ

Bring water to a boil. Add macaroni slowly, reduce heat, and cook until tender. Add cheese, eggs, and salt and pepper to taste. Pour in oiled 2-quart casserole. Bake covered for 20 minutes at 325° (or until eggs are set). Mix together bread crumbs and wheat germ and sprinkle over casserole; set casserole under broiler 3 inches from heat source until a golden crust forms. Serves 3 to 4.

Lentil-Mushroom Stew

1½ quarts stock or water
2 cups lentils, washed
1 onion, sliced and chopped
½ pound mushrooms, sliced
1 teaspoon dried basil
½ teaspoon salt

2 stalks celery and tops, chopped
2 carrots, sliced
1 can stewed tomatoes
⅓ cup oil
2 tablespoons vinegar

Bring stock to a boil and slowly add lentils. Reduce to a simmer and cook 1 hour. Meanwhile sauté onion, mushrooms, and basil in oil. Set aside. Combine all ingredients, except vinegar and seasonings, and cook at least 1 more hour, or until lentils are tender. Add vinegar before serving. Add salt and pepper to taste. Serves 4 well.

This can be served over Simple Brown Rice (see page 66).

Split Pea–Vegetable Stew

1½ quarts stock
2 cups split peas
⅓ cup barley
3 stalks celery, chopped
1 onion, sliced and chopped
greens, chopped, are good
(optional)

2 potatoes, peeled and cubed
1 bay leaf
1 clove garlic, minced
⅓ cup oil
½ teaspoon salt
2 teaspoons caraway seeds

Bring stock to a boil and slowly add split peas and barley. Reduce to simmer and cook 1 hour. Meanwhile sauté vegetables, bay leaf, and garlic in the oil. Combine with stew, add salt, and cook about 1 more hour. Add caraway seeds and simmer 30 minutes longer. Serves 4.

Yogurt

1 heaping cup of noninstant
powdered milk
½ cup evaporated milk
2 tablespoons fresh yogurt
(preferably from a natural
food store)

3 cups warm water, or enough
to fill blender after other
ingredients added

Blend all the ingredients well, pour in quart, screw-top glass jars, and place in an electric incubator. (See the

Notes, page 111). Incubation time varies from 4 to 6 hours. The yogurt is done when it can be separated with a knife, as with custard.

To make a homemade incubator, use a box and an electric heating pad, or place the jars in a pan of warm water in an oven that is kept warm by the pilot light. Homemade incubation is not always successful.

To use pasteurized or homogenized milk, you must first heat the milk to just below boiling. Cool to lukewarm before adding the starter. Yogurt is commonly served with fruit. We would like to suggest topping your serving of yogurt with 1 or 2 teaspoons of raw wheat germ and 2 or 3 tablespoons of honey, or more if you favor it sweeter.

Meat, Fowl, and Fish

In spite of the move toward vegetarian diets, meat consumption is at an all-time high in this country and shows no immediate sign of decreasing. Given this fact, and our own feeling that a healthy diet should contain some meat, fowl, and fish, we have included a variety of recipes in this area. At the same time, we are obligated to express our concern and dissatisfaction with the inferior conditions under which these animals have been raised (see the Introduction).

When cooking meats, fish, or fowl, it is best to use a low temperature which allows the connecting tissues to break down evenly as the heat penetrates. Juices are lost as the meat becomes hotter. After the meat becomes 170°F, protein begins to get tough and dry. Another way to avoid drying meat is to add salt in the last part of the cooking period. Salt draws out the juices and should be used only when this is desired, as for stew or soups. Coat very lean meat and chicken with oil before roasting to hold in the juices.

One man to know is your butcher. Become acquainted with him. Ask him questions about his meat and make him feel like an authority, which in many ways he is. Don't hesitate to select exactly the piece you want. Look it over carefully before you buy it. When, after careful preparation, it doesn't meet your expectations, tell him. If you are always as certain to tell him when the meat is good, you will have a friend.

Potato-Prune Roast

1¾ pounds of chuck roast	2 or 3 potatoes, peeled and
juice of 1 lemon	chopped (1 to 2 inches)
3 tablespoons natural sugar	3 or 4 carrots, chopped same
1 (1-pound) package prunes	size as potatoes

Trim some of the fat from the meat. Put fat in pan and brown meat slowly in this fat. Then add enough water to cover ⅝ of the meat. Add lemon, sugar, and prunes. Reduce heat and simmer 2 to 3 hours, depending on thickness of meat. Remove meat, put vegetables in pot, place meat on top, cover, and put in 325° oven for 1 more hour, or until vegetables are tender.

This is a dish that needs an ample amount of juice, so watch to see that it does not get dry. Wonderful the next day. Serves 6 to 8.

Norwegian Meatballs

¾ cup milk
1½ cups bread crumbs
3 teaspoons finely minced
   onion
2 tablespoons oil
2 pounds ground beef

1 egg
salt and pepper
¼ teaspoon nutmeg
1 can consommé, or 1½ cups
   beef stock

Mix milk and crumbs to soak. Sauté onion in oil. Remove from skillet and mix together all the ingredients, except the consommé. Shape into small balls, about 1 inch in diameter. Brown well on all sides in hot oil. Heat consommé in deep pot and, as meatballs finish browning, place them in the hot consommé. Simmer for approximately 30 minutes over low heat.

Sweet and Sour Stew

1 pound stewing beef
3 tablespoons oil
2 cups water
1 onion, sliced
salt and pepper
4 carrots, chopped in 1-inch
   pieces

½ pound mushrooms, sliced
⅓ cup catsup
¼ cup red-wine vinegar
¼ cup natural sugar
1 tablespoon Worcestershire
   sauce

Trim meat and cut into 1-inch pieces. Brown well in hot oil. Reduce heat and add 1 cup water. Add onion, salt, and pepper. Simmer 1½ hours. Add carrots and mushrooms. Combine catsup, vinegar, sugar, Worcestershire sauce, and remaining water and add to meat. Simmer together for 1 more hour, or until meat is tender. Serve over soy or wheat noodles (homemade pasta is nice). Serves 4 to 6.

Skewered Veal

2 pounds veal steak, cut in 1-inch squares
1 pound large, fresh mushrooms, washed
⅓ cup soy sauce
⅓ cup lemon juice
⅓ cup oil
1 clove garlic, mashed

Skewer veal alternately with mushrooms. Mix soy sauce, lemon, oil, and garlic. Marinate meat in this mixture for 4 to 6 hours. Broil in a hot oven for 10 to 12 minutes, or over coals for 15 to 20 minutes, until golden. Baste while broiling. Serve with Barley-Mushroom Pilaf (see page 67).

Stuffed Cabbage

1 very large cabbage

SAUCE:

⅔ onion, sliced thin
3 tablespoons oil
1 medium can tomatoes
½ teaspoon paprika
½ teaspoon dill weed
salt and pepper
juice of 1 lemon

STUFFING:

½ pound bulk pork sausage
1 clove garlic, mashed
salt and pepper
2 cups cooked rice
2 eggs
1 teaspoon paprika
½ teaspoon thyme

Remove 12 to 14 whole cabbage leaves carefully, and steam on rack above 1 cup water until leaves are tender and bend without tearing.

Prepare sauce by sautéing the onion in oil. Add the rest of the sauce ingredients, the water from the cabbage leaves, and the remaining part of the cabbage, sliced thin. Simmer for 20 to 30 minutes.

Brown the sausage and garlic with salt and pepper. Mix meat with rice, eggs, paprika, and thyme.

Spoon 1 or 2 tablespoons stuffing into the center of each cabbage leaf and roll up tightly. Place carefully in deep kettle and cover with sauce. Cover and simmer for 45 minutes to 1 hour. Serves 5 to 6.

Beef Stew

2 to 3 pounds chuck steak	1 bay leaf
1 cup whole-wheat flour	4 medium carrots, sliced
2 to 3 cups water	1 medium onion, quartered
2 tablespoons tomato paste	1 large potato, quartered
salt and pepper	1 large turnip, quartered
1 clove garlic	

Cut steak into stew-sized pieces. Trim fat and retain bone. Dredge in ⅓ cup flour and brown in heavy stew pan over moderate heat. Include bone. Add water, tomato paste, salt and pepper, garlic, and bay leaf. Simmer 1 hour. Add vegetables, except turnip, which is added the last 20 minutes. Simmer until tender. Add more flour for desired thickness. Serves 6.

Sauerbraten

4 cups cider vinegar	6 bay leaves
4 cups water	6 peppercorns
3 onions, sliced thin	3 tablespoons salt
1 lemon, sliced thin	1- to 6-pound beef rump roast
12 whole cloves	3 tablespoons oil

To prepare: Make a marinade by mixing all the ingredients, except the meat and oil, in a large bowl. Add roast; turn once or twice and cover. Refrigerate for 24 to 28 hours. Turn meat in marinade occasionally.

To cook: Use a heavy, deep pan. Remove meat and shake off marinade. Brown well in hot oil over medium heat. Add 2 cups of strained marinade and simmer, covered, for 4 to 5 hours. Remove meat and thicken juice with enough flour to make a gravy. Slice meat and serve with noodles and gravy. Serves 8 to 10.

Marinated Beef Tongue

1 beef tongue, 2 or 3 pounds	1 clove garlic, mashed
2 cups vegetable stock	½ cup sliced mushrooms
½ cup oil	2 tablespoons oil
½ cup lemon juice	½ cup tomato juice or sauce
½ onion, sliced thin	salt and pepper to taste
1 teaspoon fresh, finely chopped parsley	1 teaspoon sherry

To cook tongue: Scrub tongue with a brush and place on a rack above 2 cups vegetable stock. Steam gently for 2 to 3 hours, or until tender. Remove while hot and trim gristle at the base of the tongue. Remove the entire skin. (It is easier to remove the skin while hot.) Slice diagonally at the tip and parallel at the base from the outside toward the middle.

Marinate slices in ½ cup oil and lemon juice for 1 hour. Sauté onion, parsley, garlic, and mushrooms in remaining oil. Add tomato juice. Add tongue, lemon marinade, and seasoning and simmer together for 12 to 15 minutes. Add sherry just before serving. Serve tongue and sauce in large soup bowls with noodles. Serves 5 to 6.

Lamb Loaf

½ cup chopped onion
⅓ cup fresh, minced parsley
1 clove garlic, mashed
1 tablespoon oil
1 egg
¼ cup wheat germ

1 pound ground lamb
½ teaspoon salt
½ teaspoon dried dill weed
pepper
1 slice bread, soaked in water
  and squeezed dry

Sauté onion, parsley, and garlic in oil. Mix all ingredients together and shape into a loaf. Bake at 325° for 1 hour. Serves 4 to 5.

NOTE: Beef may be used instead of lamb.

Sweetbreads Italian

1 pound sweetbreads
1 quart water
1 tablespoon vinegar
½ pound mushrooms, sliced
¾ cup fresh, chopped parsley
1 clove garlic, minced

3 tablespoons butter
1 teaspoon dried oregano
½ cup Madeira wine
2 tablespoons Worcestershire
  sauce
salt and pepper

To prepare: Soak sweetbreads for 30 minutes in cold water to cover. Change water once. Drain and place in saucepan. Add 1 quart of cold water and 1 tablespoon vinegar and bring slowly to a boil. Reduce heat and simmer for 5 minutes. Drain well and break into sections. Remove excess cartilage and tissues, but leave fragile membrane around smaller sections.

To cook: Sauté mushrooms and parsley and garlic in butter for 4 to 5 minutes. Add sweetbreads and sauté another 4 to 5 minutes. Add oregano and liquids and simmer gently 10 to 15 minutes. Salt and pepper to taste. Serve over or alongside a grain dish (see pages 65–68).

NOTE: Watch simmering time and do not overcook.

London Lamb Kidneys

6 lamb kidneys, with sur-
rounding fat left on (if
possible)
¾ teaspoon thyme

¼ cup fresh, minced parsley
salt and pepper
lemon wedges

Wipe kidneys, do not wash. Slice, but not too thin so they
will not cook too rapidly. In a heavy skillet, sauté the
kidneys in their own fat if possible, with thyme, until
just slightly pink inside. Sprinkle with parsley and serve
immediately, with lemon wedges.

NOTE: If kidneys are without fat, use 2 tablespoons of
light oil and 2 tablespoons of butter.

Beef Heart with Ala Stuffing

1 average beef heart, 4 to 5
pounds
1 clove garlic
2 teaspoons pepper
3 tablespoons oil
5 cups vegetable stock or
bouillon
2 slices bacon (optional)
2 cups ala (bulgur wheat)

½ teaspoon salt
½ cup each of chopped onion,
celery, and carrot
1 tablespoon fresh, chopped
parsley
½ teaspoon dried thyme
½ teaspoon dried rosemary
whole-wheat flour

Trim heart of fat and remove inside connective mem-
branes. Wipe with damp cloth. Rub both sides with garlic,
pepper, and 1 tablespoon oil. Place on rack in deep kettle
over 2 cups vegetable stock. Place pieces of cut-up bacon
over heart and steam gently until tender, about 2 to 3
hours. Do not overcook.

To prepare stuffing: Bring 3 cups vegetable stock or

water to a boil. Add ala and salt. Reduce heat and simmer 15 to 20 minutes. Meanwhile, sauté onion, celery, and carrot in remaining oil for approximately 4 to 5 minutes. Mix with seasonings and cooked ala.

Place stuffing on bottom of a baking dish. Remove heart and place over stuffing. Cover with foil. Bake in preheated 350° oven for 20 to 30 minutes. Retain broth from heart and thicken with enough whole-wheat flour for gravy. Slice heart thin for serving and pour the gravy over the meat. Serves 6.

After steaming, heart can also be ground for a quick meat loaf; or it can be sliced thin, breaded, and fried quickly in vegetable oil.

African Chicken with Hot Greens

1 medium fryer, cut up
1 large bunch mustard or
    collard greens
1 large onion

1½ cups water, boiling
2 chicken bouillon cubes
10 small, red, dried chili peppers

Brown chicken well in its own fat. Use heavy, deep pan and brown slowly. Meanwhile cut up greens coarsely. Slice onion fine.

Make a broth of water, bouillon, diced heart and liver of chicken, and peppers. Grind the peppers between fingers, being certain to wash hands well afterward to avoid smarting. Simmer.

When chicken is well browned, pour ¼ of sauce over chicken and reduce heat. Lay ¾ sliced onion over chicken, then the greens over the onion, followed by the remaining onion. Pour remaining sauce over all. Cover and steam until done, about 1½ hours, without stirring. Serve with a grain (see pages 65–68). Serves 4 to 6.

Liver Sautéed in Wheat Germ

6 tablespoons oil
1 large onion, sliced thin
1 cup wheat germ
⅓ cup grated Parmesan
cheese (optional)

salt and pepper to taste
1 pound baby beef liver, sliced
thin

Heat 3 tablespoons oil in heavy skillet and sauté onion until clear. Remove and set aside. Mix wheat germ, Parmesan, salt and pepper. Heat remaining oil in pan. Dredge liver in wheat germ mixture and sauté over low heat until cooked through. Serves 4 to 5.

Sweet and Sour Chicken

1 medium fryer, cut up
½ cup wine vinegar
½ cup soy sauce
2 garlic cloves, mashed
salt and pepper

1 teaspoon prepared mustard
¾ cup catsup
⅓ cup honey or ½ cup natural
sugar

Wash and dry fryer. Put in 2-quart casserole and cover with sauce made of remaining ingredients. Cover and bake at 325° for 2 hours, or until very tender. Turn frequently while baking. Serves 4 to 5.

Grecian Chicken

1 medium fryer, cut up
2 tablespoons oil
salt and pepper

2 cups tomato sauce
½ cup sliced black olives
2 teaspoons cinnamon

Wash and dry chicken. Brown well in oil in heavy skillet.

Salt and pepper to taste. Mix tomato sauce, olives, and cinnamon. Combine chicken and sauce in a covered oven dish. Bake at 325° for 1½ to 2 hours, turning occasionally. Chicken is done when meat falls away from the bone.

Chicken Cacciatore

1 (3-pound) chicken, cut up	salt and pepper to taste
3 tablespoons oil	1 bell pepper, cut up
½ medium onion	6 large mushrooms, sliced
2 cloves garlic	½ cup tomato sauce
½ cup fresh, chopped parsley	1 cup water
½ cup butter, melted	

Fry chicken in hot oil until brown. Do not cook through. Arrange chicken in baking dish. Chop onion, garlic, and parsley until fine, add to melted butter, and sauté lightly. Pour over chicken. Add salt and pepper. Add bell pepper and mushrooms to top of chicken. Pour tomato sauce and water over top and bake 1 hour at 350°.

Sesame Fish

2 pounds fish fillets, sole, halibut, cod, snapper, or other	½ cup bread crumbs
	4 tablespoons sesame seeds
	⅓ cup oil
salt and pepper	⅓ cup fresh, chopped parsley
1 egg	¼ cup lemon juice
2 tablespoons evaporated milk	1 small onion, chopped fine
½ cup flour	

Season fish with salt and pepper. Beat egg and milk together. Dip each fillet lightly into flour, then into liquid, then into bread crumbs and seeds mixed together.

Heat oil hot, reduce heat, and fry 3 to 8 minutes, depending on thickness of fish. Absorb excess oil by draining on paper towels. Combine parsley, lemon juice, and onion and pour over fish before serving. Serves 5 to 6.

Squid Adriatic

If you have squid which has not been cleaned, it is best to have someone show you how to clean it. If you live by a wharf, a fish vendor can show you.

1 cup thinly sliced onion	1 teaspoon dried oregano
2 large cloves garlic, mashed	4 cups canned tomatoes,
4 tablespoons olive oil	coarsely chopped. If fresh are
1 cup fresh, chopped parsley	used, add 1 or 1½ cups water
1 medium bell pepper, sliced	1 teaspoon salt
thin	3 cups sliced mushrooms
1 teaspoon fresh, chopped	3 or 4 pounds cleaned squid
tarragon, or ⅓ teaspoon	2 cups water
dried	

Sauté onion and 1 clove garlic lightly in 2 tablespoons oil. Add parsley and pepper and sauté 3 to 5 more minutes, retaining 2 tablespoons of parsley for the squid. Add rest of the sauce ingredients and simmer 1½ hours.

To cook squid: Squid should be cooked separately as it has a lot of water which can cause the broth to be too fishy. Do not cut up squid. Steam above 2 cups of water for 15 minutes, or until it turns pink. Overcooking will cause squid to become tough. While steaming, pour over it a mixture of 2 tablespoons oil, 2 tablespoons parsley, and 1 clove garlic, mashed.

Put steamed squid in the hot sauce and serve immediately in flat soup bowls alongside Polenta (see page 68). Make double recipe of Polenta. Serves 8.

Barley-Stuffed Squid

12 (1½ pounds) squid bodies, still in tube form
⅔ cup chopped onion
⅓ cup fresh, chopped parsley
⅓ pound mushrooms, chopped

2 cloves garlic, mashed
3 tablespoons oil
tentacles, chopped small
2½ to 3 cups cooked barley
1 teaspoon dried basil
½ cup white wine

Steam squid bodies as directed in recipe for Squid Adriatic (see page 54). Sauté onion, parsley, mushrooms, and garlic in oil. Add tentacles 3 to 4 minutes later and sauté 3 to 4 more minutes.

Mix barley with sautéed vegetables and basil. Stuff bodies and place side by side in a flat oven dish. Cover with wine and foil. Bake at 350° for 15 to 20 minutes. Serves 4 to 5.

Rock Cod in Egg Batter

1 pound rock cod
2 eggs
½ teaspoon dried oregano
¼ teaspoon cumin
salt and pepper

1 teaspoon dried dill weed
1 clove mashed garlic
pinch of cayenne
4 tablespoons oil
lemon wedges

Cut rock cod in serving-sized pieces. Rock cod is generally cut in thicker fillets than other fish. Beat together all the remaining ingredients, except the oil and lemon, to make batter. Heat oil in heavy skillet. Dip fish in batter and

fry 5 to 6 minutes on one side. Turn and fry until flaky.
During the last few minutes, pour remaining batter over
the fish and cook without stirring, as for an omelet. Serve
with lemon wedges. Serves 4.

Curried Oysters and Corn

1 pound oysters	2 eggs, slightly beaten
2 tablespoons oil	1¼ teaspoons curry powder
2 tablespoons butter	½ cup bread crumbs
½ cup chopped onion	½ cup grated cheese
2½ cups creamed corn	

Cut oysters in bite-sized pieces. Heat oil and butter and
sauté onion and oysters briefly, about 4 to 5 minutes. Remove and boil down remaining liquid. Add corn. Place
in small, greased casserole. Stir in beaten eggs, curry
powder, oysters, and onions. Cover with crumbs and bake
for 20 to 25 minutes at 350°. Sprinkle on cheese the last
few minutes. Serves 4.

Grain Dishes

Learning about grains is fun for most people who are interested in cooking as well as baking. Once you have a knowledge of the variety of available grains, you will enjoy browsing in natural food stores. A few grain forms are sold in supermarkets — bulgur wheat (ala), kasha (buckwheat groats), rolled oats, converted rice, and, in some stores, natural brown rice. Learn to use grains as substitutes for potatoes, white-flour pastas, and white rice. All of these products can be purchased by mail order (see Notes, page 111).

WHOLE WHEAT Whole-wheat grains, or wheat berries, are a wonderful accompaniment to meat, fish, and fowl. They can also be prepared as a pilaf with vegetables as a main dish. The texture is chewy. Whole wheat is a good source of B vitamins and minerals.

BULGUR WHEAT Bulgur wheat is that which has been prepared for cooking by cracking, steaming, and toasting. It is valuable because of its high nutritional content in relation to its short preparational period. Often found packaged in supermarkets under the name *ala* because of its popularity with some ethnic groups, it is also sold in bulk in natural food stores.

OATS The Scots have eaten oats for centuries and probably brought them to this country. Breakfast oatmeal is an old favorite in the United States. Old-fashioned rolled oats require very little cooking to be palatable and are a good hearty breakfast for children, especially when sprinkled with a little wheat germ. Natural food stores and grain supply houses offer oat groats, unhulled oats, and steel-cut oats. They can be used for more textured cereals, as well as additions to breads, cookies, and muffins. Steamed oat flakes are sold in supermarkets as quick-cooking oats. They contain slightly less nutritional value.

RYE Introduced to the American diet by European immigrants, rye is a staple grain in northern Europe and Russia. It is a hardy grain which can be grown in any soil. Many nutritionists think it tends to create stronger muscles than wheat. It can be purchased in the whole grain for home grinding, or in grits to use as a cereal or in breads.

CORN Corn is native to the Americas and a staple of Mexico and some South American countries. It is a good source of inositol, a B vitamin. Do avoid refined commercial cornmeal, which contains little nutritional value and has been prepared from sterile hybrid corn. Instead purchase coarse ground cornmeal from natural food stores. It is also sold whole for home grinding and popping.

RICE   The United States has become a strong producer of rice, although most rice consumed today has been processed like wheat, with the outer husk and germ removed, leaving only starch. Natural, brown rice certainly is preferable in nutrition and tastes better. The "converted" rice in the markets is said to have been processed in a manner which forces the vitamins into the center of the rice, thus saving them from being lost in the chaff during milling. Rice polish and rice bran are the outer layers of the rice when natural rice is converted to white. The polishings, especially, are nice additions to baked goods and cereals. It is interesting to note that wild rice is considered twice as nutritious as brown rice. Unfortunately, it is expensive and not readily available.

BARLEY   Barley is another Eastern European grain. The pearl barley found in markets today is mostly starch, so we recommend buying the hulled or unhulled variety from mills or natural food stores. Barley grits are also available. Barley is a good addition to soups and casseroles, and makes a tasty rice substitute.

BUCKWHEAT   Buckwheat is a plant whose seeds are hulled and cracked for quick preparation. Sold under the term *groats* or the ethnic name *kasha*, it has a very different, hearty taste and is a good source of B vitamins. Use it as a side dish for meats and in casseroles. It is excellent with pot roast and gravy.

MILLET   This grain is a staple in many African countries and a favorite of the legendary Hunzas. A good source of protein, calcium, and lecithin, it cooks fast and is easily digestible. Use millet as a side dish, a cereal, a pudding, or in soup or bread. It also comes in meal form.

WHEAT GERM   In the center of the wheat kernel is the embryo, or germ, of the wheat which contains most of the vitamins and minerals. Extracted and sold separately, the germ is especially rich in vitamin E, but, because of its high oil content, it must be kept refrigerated to prevent rancidity. Use it on yogurt, on cereals, in baked goods and casseroles, and for breading.

Many nutritious cereal preparations are found in natural food stores, and they are beginning to appear in supermarkets.

Familia

3 cups quick oats
1½ cups raw or toasted wheat germ
1 (8-ounce) package dried apricots, cut up
1 cup chopped nuts
3 cups rolled wheat or wheat flakes
2 cups raisins
1 cup natural sugar (optional)

Mix everything together and store in jars in the refrigerator. You may substitute or add any dried fruits or nuts available. Any flaked grain may be used, such as bran, rye, etc. Familia is to be eaten raw with milk and honey.

Crunchy Dry Cereal

3 cups rolled oats
1 cup wheat germ
1 cup sesame seeds
1 cup shredded, unsweetened
  coconut

¼ cup oil
¾ cup honey
1 teaspoon vanilla
dash of salt

Mix all ingredients. Spread ½ inch deep on cookie sheet. Bake at 250° until golden brown. Stir occasionally, as sides brown first. Let cool. Store in jars. Serve with milk.

Seven-Grain Dry Cereal

3 cups rolled bran
3 cups millet flour
3 cups oatmeal
3 cups cornmeal
1½ cups whole-wheat flour
1 cup wheat germ

½ cup soy grits
1 tablespoon salt
3½ cups milk or soy milk
1½ cups dry malt
4 tablespoons honey

Blend all ingredients together except milk, malt, and honey. Mix these separately, and add to the rest to make a stiff dough. Roll out very thin. Prick with a fork and place on a greased baking sheet. Bake at 300° until golden brown. Cool and put through a food chopper or crumble with hands.

Cream of Rice

1 teaspoon oil
1 cup brown rice

2 cups water
1 teaspoon salt

To prepare: Heat the oil in a heavy skillet. Sauté rice until golden brown. The oil is only to prevent sticking. Put rice into a blender and grind into a meal at high speed. Store in the refrigerator or use immediately. You can make a much larger quantity for future use (add a little more water if needed).

To cook: Bring 2 cups of water to a boil. Add rice and salt. Reduce heat to low and simmer until desired thickness is reached, approximately 30 minutes. Stir frequently.

Millet Porridge

½ cup millet   ¾ teaspoon salt
1 cup water

Soak millet overnight in water. Bring to a boil in the morning, add salt, and cook, covered, for 20 minutes in the top of a double boiler. Mixture will be thick and can be thinned with water or hot milk if desired. Serve with honey and milk. Serves 3 to 4.

Oat Porridge

½ cup steel-cut oats   ½ teaspoon salt
2½ cups water

Pour oats slowly into boiling salted water. Cover and simmer 30 minutes. Add more water if necessary for desired consistency. Serve with honey and milk. Serves 3 to 4.

Cornmeal Mush

1 cup cornmeal   2 teaspoons salt
3½ or 4 cups milk or water,
    or mixture of both

Combine meal with 1 cup cold liquid. When smooth, add
the rest of the liquid (either boiling water or scalded
milk). Add salt and cook 30 minutes in top of a double
boiler, stirring occasionally. Milk makes the most nour-
ishing porridge for children. Serve with honey and milk.
Serves 3 to 4.

Kasha (Buckwheat Groats)

1 cup buckwheat groats   2 cups boiling water
1 egg, slightly beaten   ½ teaspoon salt

Put groats and egg in a skillet. Stir constantly over a high
heat. After each grain is separate and dry, add boiling
water and salt, and reduce heat. Cover tightly and steam
for 30 minutes. Serve with butter and salt to taste. Serves
3 to 4.

Ala (Bulgur Wheat)

1 cup bulgur wheat   2 cups stock or water
1 teaspoon oil

Sauté bulgur in oil until the grains are slightly browned.
Reduce heat and add stock slowly. Cover and simmer for
15 minutes, or until grain has absorbed the liquid. Serves
3 to 4. You can add any vegetables to make a pilaf.

Whole Wheat

6 cups water or consommé   2 teaspoons salt
2 cups whole wheat

Bring liquid to a boil. Add wheat slowly. Reduce heat and simmer very gently 3 to 4 hours, or until wheat is tender. Watch the liquid. Add salt the last hour. Serve with butter or soy sauce. It will be chewier than rice. Serves 4 to 6.

Simple Brown Rice

4 cups water   1 teaspoon salt
2 cups rice

Bring water to a boil. Add rice slowly. Reduce heat and add salt. Simmer for 1 hour, or until tender. Serve with butter or soy sauce. Serves 4 to 6.

Brown Rice Baked in Consommé

½ cup chopped onion   2 cups brown rice
⅓ cup fresh, chopped parsley   4 cups consommé or bouillon
4 tablespoons oil

Sauté onion and parsley in the oil in heavy skillet. Add rice and sauté again lightly. Remove from heat and add broth. Pour into 2-quart casserole and bake at 325° for 1 hour, or until tender. Serves 4 to 6.

Brown Rice Burgers

3 cups cooked brown rice
½ bunch parsley, chopped
3 raw carrots, grated
1 large onion, chopped
1 clove garlic, mashed

salt and pepper
1 egg
½ cup whole-wheat flour
3 to 4 tablespoons oil

Mix all ingredients except oil together until well blended. Add more flour if mixture is too soft to form patties. Put oil on hands and form patties. Fry in oil.

Can be served hot or cold. They keep well in refrigerator and make a good substitute for sandwiches in school lunches.

Barley-Mushroom Pilaf

2 cups diced mushrooms
1 tablespoon fresh, finely
   chopped parsley
1 small onion, diced
2 cups barley

½ cup oil
4 cups chicken broth
salt and pepper
1 bay leaf

Sauté mushrooms, parsley, onion, and barley in oil. Put into a 2-quart casserole with broth and seasonings, and cover. Bake at 350° for 45 minutes, or until barley is tender and liquid is absorbed. Serves 4 to 6.

Millet Hunza Style

Cook millet according to directions for Millet Porridge (see page 64). Mix with ¾ cup sautéed onion and/or top with grated cheese. Serves 3 to 4.

Millet Soufflé

1¾ cups cooked millet
½ teaspoon salt
pepper
3 egg yolks, beaten

⅔ cup milk
½ cup grated cheese
3 egg whites, stiffly beaten

Mix all ingredients together, reserving ¼ cup cheese for the top and folding in stiffly beaten egg whites last. Pour in greased baking dish and top with grated cheese. Put dish in pan of hot water and bake in moderate oven until it sets, approximately 20 minutes. Serves 4 to 5.

Polenta

For use with a meat or fish soup or stew.

1 cup cornmeal
1 cup water
1 teaspoon salt
1 teaspoon paprika

dash of cayenne
¾ cup grated cheese
½ cup meat or fish sauce

In top of a double boiler combine cornmeal, water, and salt, adding cornmeal very slowly to avoid lumping. Mix well, add paprika and cayenne, and steam over low heat for 30 minutes. Turn into an oiled baking dish or casserole and bake at 350° for 10 to 15 minutes. Top with grated cheese and/or ½ cup of sauce from the meat or fish dish. Broil until a brown crust is formed. Serves 4 to 5.

VARIATION: Drop by spoonfuls into a broth or soup.

Whole-Wheat Pasta

3 eggs   1½ teaspoons salt
4 cups sifted whole-wheat   3 to 6 tablespoons water
   flour

To prepare: Beat eggs well. Sift flour into a heap on a large, clear surface, and make a well in the middle. Put eggs and salt in the well and mix, adding water a little at a time to keep the dough soft for working. Keep sprinkling flour onto the egg, mixing all the time until the eggs and flour are well mixed. Transfer to a floured board and knead well for 10 minutes. When dough is light and elastic, divide into three to four parts. Roll out each part very thin into a rectangle and then roll them up like jelly rolls. Let dry for 30 minutes. Cut into thin strips.

To cook: Use a large kettle nearly full of boiling, well-salted water. Add pasta and continue to boil until the pasta is done to your taste. You can add a little oil to the water to prevent sticking.

Breads & Quick Breads

We have already discussed the major grains available in the United States today. All of these are ground into flours and meals for baking and breading, and broken into grits for adding to casseroles and cereals. Many flour and meal labels say "stone-ground," which indicates that the milling was done on a soft buhrstone, an age-old process which involves a slow grinding of the entire grain. After the industrial revolution, for expedience and volume, this method was almost totally replaced by fast roller mills in which the vital germ — containing 90% of the nutrients — was discarded because it became rancid from the heat of these high-speed mills and tended to stick in the machinery. Along with the extraction of the germ, chemical bleaches were added to make the flour whiter. For years, the public has been deluded into thinking this flour is somehow "nicer" than the heavier whole-grain flours.

In the last fifty years, however, many milling machines have been developed which equal the output of the roller mills without extracting the germ from the flour. These new machines spread the germ evenly throughout the flour. What we want to stress is that there is no argument left for refined flours. When the ground germ is spread evenly in the flour, the problem of rancidity is not a real danger if the flour is packaged tightly and not allowed to sit in humid areas. It is best to refrigerate whole-grain flours, especially whole wheat, after opening the package, if you need to store the flour for any length of time. It is wise to watch for flours which are milled nearby and to patronize natural food stores and markets where there is a good turnover in flour. You can also freeze flour if you wish to purchase it in large quantities. Flours and grains can be obtained by mail order (see Notes, page 111).

Before experimenting with too many flours and grains, we suggest you learn the basics of baking. The lightness of bread depends not only on the leavening, but also on the level of gluten or wheat protein in the flour. When flour is kneaded or stirred, the gluten forces the flour to stick together in thin elastic sheets and catch the gas from the yeast. This process makes the bread rise. Wheat flour contains the most gluten and rye flour has some gluten, but all other flours lack this element and tend to neutralize its effect. The germ of the wheat grain has no gluten; therefore, you should add the nonwheat flours and chaffs last, after the yeast has had a chance to work with the gluten.

In making your own bread recipes, it is wise to make a sponge first. Dissolve the yeast in lukewarm liquid and then add all the liquid required in the recipe, the sweetener, and about 2 to 3 cups of the flour containing gluten. It should be the consistency of waffle batter. Mix well, cover with a damp cloth, and set in a warm place. Let it rise for 1 hour. Stir again and add the remaining ingredients. Then cover and allow the dough to rise double. A sponge encourages quick rising and is especially effective with heavy flours.

We strongly suggest using gluten flour in bread that calls for soy flour, since soy flour is heavy and needs the effect of gluten. Gluten flour is produced by a process which washes the gluten out of the whole-wheat flour. The remainder, or gluten, is dried and ground into flour. It is sold in natural food stores and mills.

It is a good idea to add powdered milk to your baked goods for extra protein. When you are substituting honey or molasses for sugar in your own recipes, reduce by one third the amount called for.

When making quick breads, it is important to understand the leavening agents. Baking soda is considered to destroy B vitamins in whole-wheat flour and should be avoided. We have substituted baking powder for soda in our recipes, although there is a little bicarbonate of soda in all baking powders. When choosing a brand of baking powder, do not buy those which contain aluminum compounds.

If you wish to avoid baking powder entirely, we suggest adding to your batter 1 or 2 tablespoons of baker's yeast dissolved in lukewarm liquid. (We feel cake yeast works faster, but dry yeast which has the moisture removed is effective and does not have to be refrigerated.) Then set the batter in a warm place for 30 to 45 minutes before baking. Stiffly beaten egg whites folded in just before baking will help add lightness. Nutritional yeast also helps baked goods rise well.

YEAST BREADS

After dough is well mixed, transfer to a bread board for kneading. (While kneading, keep your hands and bread board covered with flour.) Fold dough, like an omelet, toward you and then push away with the heels of your palms. Continue this process until the dough becomes smooth and elastic. Then place dough in a well-oiled bowl, turn over once, cover, and let rise until double. Punch raised dough down, knead again, and shape into loaves. Bread pans should always be well greased; dough should touch each edge of a loaf pan to help support it as it rises.

The oven should be preheated at least 5 minutes for bread and pastry baking. Bread is done when it is golden brown. Remove the pans from the oven and turn them on their sides. After a few minutes, remove the bread from the pans and transfer the loaves to a wire rack to cool. Bread gets damp when left in pans.

High Protein Bread

3 cups warm water	3 tablespoons wheat germ
2 cakes yeast	½ cup soy flour or powder
2 tablespoons honey	¾ cup skim-milk powder
3 cups whole-wheat flour	4 teaspoons salt
4 cups unbleached flour	2 tablespoons oil or butter

Combine the water, yeast, and honey. Let stand for 5 minutes. Measure and sift the whole-wheat and unbleached flour, wheat germ, soy flour, and skim-milk powder. Stir the yeast mixture, and while stirring, add the salt and 3 cups of the flour mixture. Beat 75 strokes or 2 minutes with an electric mixer. Add the oil and 3 cups flour mixture. Blend and then turn out on a floured board, adding 1 cup or more additional flour as needed. Knead thoroughly, about 5 minutes, until dough is smooth and elastic. Place in a well-oiled bowl and let rise until double. Punch dough down, fold over the edges, and turn dough upside down. Let it rise another 20 minutes.

Turn out on a board, shape in 2 loaves, place in buttered bread pan, cover, and let rise until double. Bake at 350° for 50 to 60 minutes. If loaves begin to brown too soon, or as soon as 15 to 20 minutes, reduce heat to 325°.

This recipe makes excellent rolls.

Cracked Wheat Bread

2⅔ cups water
1½ cups cracked wheat
⅓ cup plus 1 teaspoon honey
1 teaspoon salt
2 tablespoons oil

2 cakes yeast
2½ cups gluten and/or
　unbleached flour
3 cups whole-wheat flour

Pour 2 cups boiling water over the cracked wheat. Add the honey (reserving 1 teaspoon for later), salt and oil. Cool. Dissolve the yeast in ⅔ cup warm water and add the 1 teaspoon honey. Combine with the cooled cracked-wheat mixture. Add the flour and mix thoroughly. Place in a buttered bowl and cover, and let rise for 1 hour. Punch down and let rise for another 30 minutes.

Punch down and turn out on a floured board. Knead well. Shape into 2 loaves and place in buttered loaf pans. Bake at 350° until golden brown.

Oatmeal Bread

1 cake yeast
¼ cup lukewarm water
4 cups skim milk, boiling
2 cups rolled oats
½ cup oil

½ cup molasses
1 tablespoon salt
5 cups gluten and/or
  unbleached flour
7 cups whole-wheat flour

Dissolve the yeast in the warm water. Add the skim milk to the oats and oil and let stand for 30 minutes. Add the molasses, salt, and the dissolved yeast. Add enough of the flour to make a soft dough. Put dough into a buttered bowl, cover, and let rise until double. Turn out on a floured board and knead until elastic, about 10 minutes.

Divide into three loaves and place in 9-inch loaf pans and let rise again. Brush the tops with melted butter and bake in a 400° oven for 40 to 50 minutes or until golden brown.

VARIATION: Add ½ cup honey, 1 cup raisins, and 1 cup chopped nuts before adding the flour.

Sourdough Steel-Cut Oats Bread

2½ cups water
2 cups steel-cut oats
2 tablespoons honey
2 cups unbleached flour
1½ cups Sourdough Starter
  (see page 81)
1 cake yeast
¼ cup honey

⅓ cup margarine or butter,
  melted
2 teaspoons salt
2 cups gluten and/or
  unbleached flour
3 cups graham or whole-wheat
  flour

To make sponge: Pour 2 cups boiling water over the steel-cut oats and let it stand until lukewarm. Stir in 2 tablespoons of honey, 2 cups unbleached flour, and the starter. Blend thoroughly, cover the bowl, and let stand for several hours, or in a cold room overnight.

When the sponge is ready, dissolve the yeast in ½ cup warm water and add to the sponge with the rest of the ingredients. Blend well and turn out on a floured board. Knead, adding more flour if necessary to make a firm, unsticky dough. Knead until dough is smooth and elastic. Return to bowl; brush dough with melted butter, cover, and let rise until double.

When dough is double, turn out on a floured board and knead it down. Then cut into three pieces and shape into three loaves. Place in buttered loaf pans, cover, and let rise until double. Bake in a 350° oven for 45 to 55 minutes. After loaves are golden brown, brush them with butter. Turn out on racks to cool. This bread makes wonderful toast.

Egg Bread

1½ cups milk	½ cup lukewarm water
½ cup butter or margarine	2 eggs, beaten
2 teaspoons salt	8 cups unbleached, sifted flour,
2 cakes yeast	approximate

Scald milk and add butter. Let cool. Add salt. Dissolve the yeast in the lukewarm water and let stand until it bubbles, about 5 minutes. Add the yeast and the eggs to the cooled milk. Gradually add the flour, beating it in thoroughly. Do not add any more flour than is necessary to make an easily handled dough, as the bread should be light and tender. Knead until smooth and elastic. Place in a greased bowl, cover, and let rise until double. Punch down and knead again.

Shape into loaves and place in 3 greased loaf pans. Cover and let rise until dough reaches the top of the pans. Bake at 350° for 40 minutes.

VARIATION: CINNAMON BREAD   Roll a portion of the dough 1 inch thick. Spread with melted margarine or butter and sprinkle with natural sugar and cinnamon. You may also add chopped nuts or raisins. Roll as for jelly roll and place in a greased pan with the seam at the bottom. Let rise until double and bake as for Egg Bread.

Sourdough French Bread

1 cup plus 1 tablespoon water	1½ cups Sourdough Starter (see page 81)
2 tablespoons honey	2½ cups unbleached flour
2 tablespoons margarine	2 teaspoons salt
1 cake yeast	

Mix 2 cups hot water, honey, and margarine. Cool to lukewarm. Add yeast, starter, and enough flour to make a firm dough (about 2 cups). Turn out onto a floured board and knead thoroughly. Place in a greased bowl, cover, and let rise until double. Punch dough down and let rise another 30 minutes.

Turn the dough out onto a floured board and let rest for 10 minutes before shaping. You may make a round loaf, a long thin loaf, or an oval loaf. Place on a cookie sheet sprinkled with cornmeal. Let rise until double and bake at 400° approximately 50 minutes.

The dough is usually slashed in several places with a very sharp knife just prior to baking. If a very sharp instrument is used, the bread will not fall.

To make Egg-White Glaze: The best glaze for any hard-crusted bread is an egg white beaten just to blend with 1 tablespoon cold water. Brush this on the bread several times while baking.

VARIATION: This recipe can also be used to make 12 delicious rolls. Shape the rolls after the first rising and place them on greased, cornmeal-sprinkled sheets. Cover and let rise again until double. Bake in a 400° oven for 20 minutes, or until brown.

Swedish Rye Bread

1 cup scalded milk	1 cake yeast
2½ teaspoons salt	3½ cups unbleached flour, sifted
2 tablespoons molasses	1 tablespoon caraway seeds
2 tablespoons oil	2 cups rye flour
1 cup water	

Pour the milk over the salt, molasses, and oil. Add the water. When cool, add the yeast and unbleached flour and beat until smooth. Stir in the caraway seeds. Gradually add the rye flour and mix to make a medium-stiff dough. The dough will be sticky. Turn it out onto a floured board and knead until smooth, about 10 minutes. Place in a buttered bowl, cover, and let rise until double, about 2 hours. Punch down and let rise again.

Turn out and shape into 2 oblong loaves. Place on buttered cookie sheets that have been sprinkled with cornmeal. Let rise until double. Bake in a 375° oven for 30 to 40 minutes.

Shepherds Bread

To make sponge:

1 cake or 1 package yeast	2 cups whole-wheat and 1 cup
2 cups lukewarm water	gluten and/or unbleached
2 tablespoons malt or honey	flour

Dissolve the yeast slowly in the water, and thoroughly blend in the flour and malt or honey. Cover with a clean towel and let rise in a warm place for approximately 4 hours.

To make dough:

1 cake or 1 package yeast	2 tablespoons oil
1 cup lukewarm water	2 cups gluten and/or unbleached
1 tablespoon salt	flour
2 tablespoons honey	1 cup whole-wheat flour

Dissolve the yeast in the water. Blend in the salt, honey, oil, and flour. Blend well. Thoroughly mix this into the sponge until pliable and smooth. Dough will pull away from the bowl. Turn out on a lightly floured board and knead for 3 to 5 minutes, and then let rest for 10 minutes.

Shape into one long or round loaf, cut a cross in the center, and place on a cornmeal-sprinkled baking sheet. Cover and let rise until *almost* double. Then put a pan of boiling water on the floor of the oven and place the bread in the oven. Set temperature for 400°, and bake the bread for 45 minutes, or until it is golden brown and done. Brush with Egg-White Glaze (see page 79) before and after baking.

Anadama Bread

1 cup scalded milk	2 teaspoons salt
1½ cups water	2 cakes yeast
1 cup yellow cornmeal	2 cups gluten and/or
¼ cup oil	unbleached flour
½ cup molasses	4 cups whole-wheat flour

Combine the hot milk and 1 cup boiling water and slowly add the cornmeal. Add the oil, molasses, and salt. Let stand until lukewarm. Sprinkle the yeast into ½ cup warm water and let stand until it bubbles, about 5 minutes. Stir it into the cornmeal mixture. Beat in the flour. Turn out onto a floured board and knead until smooth and elastic, about 8 minutes.

Place dough in a greased bowl, cover, and let rise until double, about 1½ hours. Knead again and divide into 2 loaves. Place in buttered loaf pans, cover, and let rise until double again. Bake at 375° for 40 to 50 minutes.

Sourdough Starter

Sourdough starters may also be purchased.

1 cake yeast	2 cups warm potato water (water
1 teaspoon natural sugar	in which potatoes have been
	cooked)

Combine all the ingredients and place in glass or pottery container. Cover with cheesecloth and let stand at room temperature for 48 hours. You may need to stir it down occasionally.

After designated time, make sponge starter by adding equal parts of water and flour (2 cups of each will generally make enough for any recipe). Stir the mixture until

well blended and let sit in a warm place for at least 8
hours. When it is ready, take 1 cup of the starter and
store, covered, in the refrigerator for later use. Then
proceed with your recipe. For large amounts of baking,
it's best to repeat this procedure rather than stretch the
starter too far.

QUICK BREADS

Stir batter only to moisten all the ingredients. Do not beat
or knead quick breads. We think soy flour works well in
muffins.

Walnut Bran Muffins

1 cup whole-wheat flour	1 egg
1/8 teaspoon salt	3/4 cup raisins (optional)
1/4 cup nonfat, powdered milk	1/3 cup honey
3 teaspoons baking powder	1 cup milk
1 cup bran	3/4 cup walnuts
1/4 cup oil	

Sift together the flour, salt, powdered milk, and baking
powder. Add and stir until mixed (but do not overmix)
the remaining ingredients. Bake at 400° for 15 minutes.
Makes 12 muffins.

Wheat Germ Muffins

1 cup gluten and/or unbleached flour	2 tablespoons honey
1 cup whole-wheat flour	1 cup milk
3 teaspoons baking powder	1/3 cup vegetable oil
1/2 teaspoon salt	1 egg
	1/2 cup wheat germ

Mix dry ingredients (except wheat germ) together. Mix

moist ingredients together and stir into dry ingredients. Add wheat germ last. Bake at 350° for 20 minutes in greased muffin tins. Makes 12 muffins.

Mexican Spoon Bread

1 small can cream-style corn
¾ cup milk
⅓ cup oil
2 eggs, slightly beaten
1 cup cornmeal

2 teaspoons baking powder
½ teaspoon salt
1 can chopped green chilies
1½ cups shredded Cheddar
　　cheese

Mix together creamed corn, milk, oil, and eggs. Add cornmeal, baking powder, and salt. Pour half of the batter into a 9 x 9-inch baking dish. Place on top a layer made of one half of the chilies and cheese. Pour on remaining batter. Top with the other half of chilies and cheese. Bake about 45 to 55 minutes at 350°.

Pumpkin Bread

1 large can pumpkin
2½ cups honey
1 cup oil
2 eggs
2½ cups whole-wheat flour,
　　sifted
2½ cups unbleached flour,
　　sifted

6 teaspoons baking powder
4 teaspoons cloves
1 teaspoon cinnamon
½ teaspoon salt
1 cup water
2 cups chopped nuts
2 cups raisins (optional)

Mix together pumpkin, honey, oil, eggs. Add dry ingredients alternately with water. Add nuts, and raisins if desired. Bake 1 hour at 350° in 3 loaf pans.

Whole-Wheat Banana Nut Bread

⅓ cup honey
½ cup oil
3 medium-sized, ripe bananas, mashed
1 teaspoon vanilla
2 eggs, well beaten

1½ cups whole-wheat flour
½ cup wheat germ
2 teaspoons baking powder
½ teaspoon salt
½ teaspoon cinnamon
½ cup coarsely cut nuts

Cream honey and oil, and stir in bananas, vanilla, and well-beaten eggs. Combine all the rest of the ingredients and stir in only until just mixed. Bake in 5 x 9-inch bread pan in 325° oven for 1 hour and 10 minutes, or until golden brown.

Corn Bread

1 cup cornmeal
1 cup unbleached flour
⅓ cup wheat germ
2 tablespoons rice polish
1 teaspoon salt

2 teaspoons baking powder
2 eggs
1½ cups buttermilk
1 tablespoon honey
¼ cup oil

Mix dry ingredients together. Add beaten eggs to buttermilk, honey, and oil and mix together. Mix liquids into the dry ingredients until just moistened. Bake in an 8 x 8 x 2-inch cake pan at 425° for 30 to 35 minutes.

Whole-Wheat Tortillas

2 cups whole-wheat flour
½ teaspoon salt

¾ to 1 cup water

Blend flour and salt. Stir in enough water to make a stiff

dough. Knead on a floured surface until smooth and elastic. Break dough into 1-inch rounds and roll into very thin tortillas. Cook over a low heat on a lightly greased griddle or frying pan. Turn one or more times. Makes 18 to 20, depending on size.

Wheat Germ Pancakes

1½ cups milk	1 cup wheat germ
2 eggs	1 teaspoon baking powder
2 cups gluten flour	1 teaspoon salt

Add milk and eggs to dry ingredients. Mix only until all ingredients are moistened. Bake on a hot griddle.

Sourdough Waffles

1 cup Sourdough Starter (see page 81)	4 tablespoons vegetable oil
2 cups water	¼ cup evaporated milk
2 cups flour (⅔ cup soy flour, ⅔ cup whole-wheat flour, ⅔ cup gluten flour recommended)	1 teaspoon salt
	1 teaspoon honey
	2 eggs, separated

The night before, mix the Sourdough Starter, the water, and the flour. Reserve, the next morning, 1 cup of this mixture as future starter and store in the refrigerator. Add the rest of the ingredients to the remaining sourdough mixture, making sure that the egg whites are stiff-beaten and added last. Spoon the batter onto a waffle iron and bake until golden brown.

VARIATION: For pancakes cut the amount of oil in half.

Coffee Cake

1¼ cups whole-wheat pastry
    flour*
¼ cup wheat germ
3 teaspoons baking powder
¼ teaspoon salt
⅓ cup honey
⅓ cup oil
⅔ cup milk
grated rind of ½ orange

½ cup orange juice
1 egg, beaten
1 cup raisins
¾ cup chopped nuts
1 teaspoon cinnamon
2 teaspoons butter
2 teaspoons natural sugar
    (not honey)

Mix together the flour, wheat germ, baking powder, and salt. Mix together the rest of the ingredients except the cinnamon, butter, and sugar and add to the flour mixture. Pour the batter into a greased 9 x 13-inch cake pan. Mix the cinnamon, butter, and sugar; crumble and sprinkle over the top. Bake at 350° for 20 to 30 minutes.

*See page 89 for a discussion of pastry and regular flours.

Desserts

Whole-wheat pastry flour, made from soft wheat, is available in some markets and all natural food stores. However, many good bakers use hard wheat bread flour for all baking. We do not often specify pastry flour in our recipes, as we simply sift hard-wheat bread flour twice, saving the chaff, or bran, for muffins and cookies, and using the sifted flour for pastry baking. Try regular pastry flour as well as our technique and see what works best for you. Flour texture varies greatly according to the mill source.

Most of the following recipes call for oil, although some ask for margarine or shortening. When buying shortening, read the labels for additives. Pure safflower oil shortening is available in some markets and in natural food stores.

Generally our dessert recipes call for honey. As with breads, when substituting honey for sugar, always use one third less honey than is specified for sugar.

Learn to use carob powder as a substitute for chocolate. Carob is much lower in starch and fat, and is richer in protein. It has a stronger flavor, so use less carob than chocolate.

A few of our recipes call for a springform (or tube) pan. They are preferable for shape and easy removal but not essential. We think an electric hand mixer is a good investment but an egg beater or wire whisk is usable with perseverance.

PIE CRUST   When making pie crust, blend shortening and flour well before adding cold water. Work very lightly after adding water, and roll with strong strokes.

COOKIES   Cookies gain nutritional value when extra powdered milk is added, but they brown quickly and should be baked at a slightly lower temperature than required in the recipe. Experiment in cookie recipes with seeds, nuts, grains, unsweetened coconut, carob powder, and fruit.

CAKES   In making cakes, the leavening is crucial. If you don't use baking powder, 1½ to 2 tablespoons dry yeast is advised, although yeast is much less effective in cakes calling for a minimum of flour. Also, along with yeast, it is advisable to add any extra egg whites you may have. Beat them stiffly and fold in last. When using honey in cakes, bake at a slightly lower temperature to insure complete baking in the center.

Spring Rhubarb Pudding

8 slices bread, toasted
1½ cups milk
¼ cup butter
5 eggs, slightly beaten
1 cup honey, or 1½ cups
   natural sugar

½ teaspoon cinnamon
¼ teaspoon salt
2 cups diced rhubarb
¾ cup wheat germ

Trim crusts from toast and cut into ½-inch cubes. Place in a buttered casserole dish. Scald milk and add butter, stirring until melted. Pour over toast cubes and allow to stand 15 minutes. Combine eggs, honey, cinnamon, salt, and rhubarb. Stir into bread mixture. Sprinkle top with wheat germ. Bake 45 to 50 minutes. While warm, spoon into serving dishes and top with half and half. Serves 8 to 10.

Old-Fashioned Baked Custard

1 quart milk
1½ teaspoons vanilla
pinch of salt
3 egg yolks

2 whole eggs
⅓ to ½ cup honey, to taste
nutmeg

Place all the ingredients except nutmeg in blender and mix well. Pour into ungreased individual custard cups. Sprinkle with nutmeg. Set the dishes in a pan of warm water in the oven. Bake at 300° until set, or when able to cut cleanly with a knife, approximately 1 hour.

Tapioca Pudding

8 tablespoons real tapioca   2 tablespoons honey
   (not large pearl)   1 teaspoon vanilla
3 cups milk

Soak tapioca in milk for 15 minutes. Cook over medium heat until thickened (8 to 10 minutes) without overcooking. Add honey and vanilla. Fresh fruit or coconut is optional. For fluffier pudding, after removing from the heat, fold in one stiffly beaten egg white. Serves 4 to 6.

Persimmon Pudding

2 teaspoons baking powder   ½ cup honey
1 cup persimmon pulp   1 egg, beaten
1 cup sifted whole-wheat flour   1 tablespoon melted butter
1 teaspoon salt   1 teaspoon vanilla
1 teaspoon cinnamon

Mix baking powder into the persimmon pulp. Mix together the dry ingredients. Add moist ingredients, a little at a time, mixing well after each addition. Bake in a covered dish for 45 to 60 minutes in a 350° oven. Serve warm or cold with cream.

Whole-Wheat Pie Crust

1 cup whole-wheat pastry   ⅔ cup shortening
   flour, sifted   ¾ teaspoon salt
1 cup unbleached flour   3 or 4 teaspoons cold water

Blend the flours and shortening. Add salt and cold water

and mix, with a minimum of strokes. Press into a ball and divide into two pieces and roll out. Place in greased pie tins and bake at 350° for 15 minutes. Watch so they don't burn.

Danish Apple Pie

6 or 7 apples, sliced
½ cup honey
½ cup margarine
1½ cups whole-wheat flour

pinch of salt
1 teaspoon cinnamon
½ cup natural sugar

Butter a baking dish. Place the apples in the dish and drizzle with honey. Mix together margarine, flour, salt, cinnamon, and sugar. Sprinkle over the apples and bake at 375° for 30 minutes.

Lemon Cheesecake

1½ cups graham-cracker
crumbs
¼ cup melted butter
2 tablespoons honey
2 cups small-curd cottage
cheese
¼ cup honey
4 eggs, separated

¼ teaspoon salt
1 teaspoon grated lemon peel
2 tablespoons lemon juice
1 teaspoon vanilla
1 cup unflavored yogurt (see
page 40)
⅓ cup honey

Mix together crumbs, butter, and 2 tablespoons honey with a pastry blender. Save aside ¼ cup of the mixture. Press remainder into bottom and ¾ way up the sides of a 10-inch springform pan, lightly greased. Bake 5 minutes at 250°.

In blender, combine cottage cheese, ¼ cup honey, egg

yolks, salt, lemon peel and juice, vanilla, and yogurt. Blend until smooth.

Beat egg whites until soft peaks form, and then gradually add the ⅓ cup of honey. Beat until stiff. Fold into the cheese mixture, mixing until smooth. Pour into the graham-cracker crust. Sprinkle the ¼-cup set-aside crumb mixture over all. Bake at 250° for 1 hour. Turn off heat and leave in the oven 1 more hour. Remove and cool thoroughly, and then chill overnight.

Strawberry Pie

1 quart strawberries, cleaned and drained
3 tablespoons arrowroot thickening starch
⅔ cup honey
½ cup boiling water
1 baked 8-inch pie shell (see page 92)
½ cup cream, whipped and sweetened

Sort berries, reserving the larger ones. Mash the small berries to make 1 cup. Blend starch, honey, and crushed berries in a small saucepan. Add boiling water and cook, stirring constantly, over medium heat until thickened and clear. Cool. Place whole berries in pie shell and pour the cooked strawberry mixture over them. Chill and serve with whipped cream.

Apple Pie

7 cups peeled and quartered apples
½ teaspoon nutmeg
¾ cup honey
½ cup plus 2 tablespoons whole-wheat pastry flour
1 unbaked pie shell (see page 92)
¼ cup lemon juice
2 tablespoons butter

Mix apples, nutmeg, ½ cup honey, and 2 tablespoons flour together well and place in unbaked pie shell. Pour lemon juice over all. Blend remaining ingredients together and sprinkle over the apple mixture. Bake at 425° for 1 hour.

Persimmon Cookies

⅔ cup honey
½ cup shortening
1 egg, well beaten
2 teaspoons baking powder
1 cup persimmon pulp

2 cups unbleached flour
1 teaspoon salt
½ teaspoon cinnamon
⅛ teaspoon powdered cloves
1 cup chopped nuts

Mix together honey, shortening, and egg. Dissolve baking powder in persimmon pulp and beat into honey mixture. Mix in dry ingredients thoroughly, stirring nuts in last. Drop by rounded teaspoons on a greased baking sheet. Bake 10 to 15 minutes at 375°.

Peanut Butter Cookies

½ cup oil
¾ cup honey
1 egg
½ cup nonhydrogenated
    peanut butter
1½ cups sifted whole-wheat
    flour

1 teaspoon baking powder
½ teaspoon salt
1½ teaspoons orange juice or
    water
1 teaspoon vanilla

Mix oil, honey, and egg thoroughly. Blend in peanut butter. Mix in flour, baking powder, and salt alternately with orange juice or water. Add vanilla. Shape into small balls and flatten with a fork dipped in flour. Then bake on a greased cookie sheet at 350° for 10 minutes.

Oatmeal Cookies

¾ cup shortening
⅔ cup honey
2 eggs
2 teaspoons vanilla
½ teaspoon salt

1 cup whole-wheat flour
2 teaspoons baking powder
3 cups oatmeal
½ cup nuts
½ cup shredded, unsweetened
  coconut

Cream shortening, honey, eggs, and vanilla together. Add salt, flour, baking powder, and oatmeal. Mix well. Add nuts and coconut and mix thoroughly. Drop by rounded teaspoons on greased cookie sheet. Bake at 325° for 10 minutes.

VARIATION: Add grated carrots, apples, or any seeds, especially poppy seeds. Cut-up dried fruits may also be added.

Crunchy Nut Cookies

½ cup honey
½ cup shortening
2 eggs
1 teaspoon vanilla

2 teaspoons baking powder
½ teaspoon salt
2½ cups whole-wheat flour
1 cup chopped nuts

Preheat oven to 375°. Mix honey, shortening, eggs, and vanilla thoroughly. Add baking powder, salt, and flour and mix well. Stir in nuts. Shape dough into small balls. Place on ungreased cookie sheet and flatten with bottom of a greased glass dipped in natural sugar. Bake 8 to 10 minutes. Makes 5 dozen.

Sour Cream Cookies

1 cup honey
1 cup shortening or butter
1 egg
1 tablespoon grated lemon
   peel

1 cup sour cream
1 teaspoon salt
1½ teaspoons baking powder
3½ cups unbleached flour
nuts or raisins

Mix honey and shortening. Add egg and lemon peel and mix well. Mix in sour cream. Add salt, baking powder, and flour and mix thoroughly. Drop by rounded teaspoons on ungreased pan. Flatten with glass dipped in natural sugar. Press in nuts or raisins. Bake at 375°. Makes 7 dozen.

Sunflower Seed Walnut Bars

1½ cups oil
1½ cups honey
6 eggs
4 teaspoons baking powder
6 cups sifted whole-wheat
   flour
drop of vanilla

2 tablespoons grated orange rind
4 tablespoons orange juice
½ cup shredded, unsweetened
   coconut
½ cup sunflower seeds
½ cup chopped walnuts

To make the bottom layer, mix ¾ cup oil, ½ cup honey, 2 eggs, 2 teaspoons baking powder, 3 cups flour, and the vanilla together and pat into a greased 9 x 13-inch pan.

For the topping, beat the 4 eggs, mix them in with the remaining ingredients, and pour over bottom layer. Bake at 325° for approximately 45 minutes. Cool and cut into squares.

Ranger Cookies

½ cup shortening
1 cup honey
1 egg
½ teaspoon vanilla
¼ teaspoon salt
1 teaspoon baking powder

½ cup shredded, unsweetened
  coconut
1 cup whole-wheat flour
1 cup oats
1 cup dry cereal flakes

Preheat oven to 350°. Mix shortening thoroughly with honey, egg, and vanilla. Stir in remaining ingredients. Drop by rounded teaspoons 2 inches apart on a greased cookie sheet. Bake 10 minutes and remove from the sheet immediately. Makes 3 dozen.

Sesame Seed Cookies

¾ cup butter or margarine
¾ cup honey
2 eggs
1 teaspoon vanilla

1¼ cups unbleached flour
½ teaspoon baking powder
½ cup sesame seeds, toasted

Thoroughly mix together butter, honey, and eggs. Add vanilla and mix again. Add all the remaining ingredients and mix well. Drop by rounded teaspoons on a greased cookie sheet. Cookies will spread, so allow space between them. Bake at 325° for 10 to 15 minutes.

Gingersnaps

1½ cups shortening
1⅓ cups honey
2 eggs
½ cup molasses
pinch of salt

2 cups whole-wheat flour
2 cups unbleached flour
2½ teaspoons baking powder
2 teaspoons each of cinnamon,
  powdered cloves, and ginger

Cream shortening, honey, and eggs. Add molasses and mix well. Add dry ingredients little by little, mixing after each addition. Roll in balls and flatten with a fork. Place on ungreased cookie sheet and bake at 350° for about 8 to 10 minutes, or until cookies are flat, cracked, and browned.

Delicious Squares

4 cups oats
1 cup sesame seeds
1 cup shredded, unsweetened
  coconut
½ cup wheat germ
½ cup nuts

dash of salt
2 cups oil
5 or 6 eggs
1 cup honey, or 2 cups natural
  sugar
1 teaspoon vanilla

Mix oats, seeds, coconut, wheat germ, nuts, and salt together and spread in bottom of a 9 x 13-inch baking pan. Mix together the oil, eggs, honey, and vanilla and pour over top of oat mixture. Bake at 350° for 30 minutes. Cut into squares while warm.

Walnut Honey Cake

1 cup milk
¾ cup honey
1¼ cups whole-wheat flour,
  sifted
1¼ cups unbleached flour,
  sifted

1 teaspoon salt
2 teaspoons baking powder
½ cup chopped nuts
2 unbeaten egg yolks, or
  1 whole egg
¼ cup butter, soft

Combine milk and honey in a 3-quart saucepan. Heat over medium heat, stirring constantly until mixed and lukewarm. Cool. Then, sift together flours, salt, and baking powder, and mix with the cooled honey and milk with an electric mixer at the lowest speed. (Can be mixed by hand.) Add nuts, egg, and butter and beat another 2 minutes at the lowest speed. Pour into 9 x 5 x 3-inch loaf pan, well greased on the bottom. Bake in 325° oven approximately 1½ hours.

Poppy Seed Cake

1½ cups poppy seeds	1½ cups dry bread crumbs
6 eggs, separated	2 teaspoons baking powder
3 tablespoons honey	¼ teaspoon salt
¾ cup honey	1 teaspoon vanilla
⅔ cup vegetable oil	

Cook poppy seeds in a pan with enough water to cover. Simmer for 15 to 20 minutes (watch water). Drain and cool. Beat egg whites until soft peaks form. Gradually add 3 tablespoons of honey. Continue beating until stiff. Set aside.

Beat the egg yolks until lemon colored. Gradually beat in the remaining honey and then the oil. Add poppy seeds. Combine the bread crumbs, baking powder, and salt. Blend into the poppy-seed mixture. Last, fold in the egg whites. Add vanilla.

Turn into greased 10-inch tube pan and bake at 325° for 1 hour. Turn out to cool.

Fresh Carrot Cake

1 teaspoon cinnamon	1½ cups grated carrots
1 teaspoon mace	3 teaspoons baking powder
½ teaspoon salt	1 cup sifted whole-wheat flour
1 cup butter or margarine	1 cup unbleached flour
1½ cups honey	1 cup hot water
4 eggs	⅔ cup chopped nuts

Blend spices and butter. Gradually add honey and beat well. Beat in eggs one at a time and stir in carrots. Sift baking powder with flour, and add alternately with hot water. Add nuts and beat well. Put into a greased 9 x 13-inch pan; ice with Honey and Cream Cheese Icing (see page 104). Bake 35 minutes at 350°, or until done.

Gingerbread

¾ cup honey	1 teaspoon salt
¾ cup oil	1½ teaspoons powdered cloves
1 cup molasses	3 teaspoons baking powder
3 eggs	1 teaspoon ginger
3 cups sifted whole-wheat flour	1½ teaspoons cinnamon
	2 cups milk

Mix honey, oil, molasses, and eggs together; set aside. Sift together all the dry ingredients. Add this flour mixture to the honey mixture alternately with the milk. Pour in greased 9 x 13-inch pan and bake at 350° for 40 minutes.

Soy-Applesauce Cake

1½ cups sifted whole-wheat
    flour
¾ cup soy flour
½ cup powdered skim milk
4 teaspoons baking powder
1 teaspoon salt
2 teaspoons cinnamon

⅔ cup honey
½ cup oil
4 eggs
¾ cup applesauce
½ cup wheat germ
1 cup raisins

Sift together dry ingredients, except wheat germ. Cream honey, oil, and eggs together. Mix dry ingredients with the creamed mixture alternately with the applesauce, wheat germ, and raisins. Beat well. Turn into a greased 9 x 13-inch cake pan and bake at 350° for 40 to 45 minutes.

Apple Spice Cake

½ cup butter
⅔ cup honey
⅓ cup cold coffee
1 egg, beaten
1 cup whole-wheat flour,
    sifted
½ cup bran

½ cup gluten and/or
    unbleached flour
1 teaspoon cinnamon
½ teaspoon powdered cloves
3 teaspoons baking powder
1 cup grated raw apple

Cream butter and honey. Add coffee, which has been mixed with the egg. Add the dry ingredients alternately with the grated apple. Pour in a greased, 8-inch-square pan and bake at 350° for 15 minutes. Lower temperature to 300° for 20 more minutes.

VARIATION: A. sprinkling of 2 teaspoons of cinnamon mixed with 3 teaspoons of natural sugar is a good addition before baking. Raisins or nuts may be added. This is also good served warm as a coffee cake.

Sour Cream Pound Cake

1 cup butter	1 cup sour cream
1 cup honey	3 cups unbleached flour, sifted
6 eggs	½ teaspoon salt
1 teaspoon almond extract	1 teaspoon baking powder

Cream butter and honey. Add eggs one at a time, beating well after each. Add extract and sour cream, again beating well. Add flour, salt, and baking powder and mix well. Place in a greased, floured springform pan. Bake at 325° for 1 to 1½ hours. Test to make sure it is done. We mix the cake with an electric mixer, but you can use an egg-beater and energy.

Oat Cake

1 egg	2 cups oats, quick or rolled
⅓ cup oil	1 cup wheat germ
½ cup honey	2 teaspoons baking powder
1 cup whole-wheat flour, sifted	⅔ cup orange juice
	1 teaspoon vanilla

Blend egg, oil, and honey. Mix in dry ingredients alternately with the juice and vanilla. Bake at 350° for about 40 minutes in an 8-inch square pan. Frost with Honey and Cream Cheese Icing (see page 104).

Sherry Wine Cake

1 cup butter or margarine	1 teaspoon nutmeg
1⅓ cups honey	pinch of salt (optional)
1½ cups gluten and/or	¾ cup oil
unbleached flour	½ cup sherry
1½ cups whole-wheat flour	1 cup almonds, or other nuts
3 teaspoons baking powder	6 egg whites, stiffly beaten

Cream the butter and honey together. Sift flour, baking powder, nutmeg, and a pinch of salt, if desired, three times. Mix flour into the butter and honey alternately with the oil and sherry. Add almonds and beat well. Carefully fold in stiffly beaten egg whites. Pour into a greased and floured springform pan. Bake in preheated 350° oven for 1 hour, or until a toothpick comes out clean when inserted in the center.

NOTE: We make this cake without nuts for a good plain cake.

Honey and Cream Cheese Icing

The following is a very good icing that may be used on any cake.

Blend honey and cream cheese until a desired consistency is reached.

Vanilla or almond or lemon extract may be added. Chopped walnuts and/or shredded coconut can be sprinkled on top after spreading the icing.

Sesame Seed Squares

½ cup honey
½ cup nonhydrogenated
    peanut butter
1 cup powdered milk

½ cup shredded, unsweetened
    coconut
1 cup sesame seeds

Heat honey and peanut butter. Add dry milk, coconut, and then seeds. Mix and pat into square pan. Refrigerate to set. Cut into squares.

Super Fudge

1 cup honey
1 cup nonhydrogenated
    peanut butter
1 cup carob powder
1 cup sesame seeds

1 cup sunflower seeds
½ cup shredded, unsweetened
    coconut
½ cup dates or other fruit

Heat honey and peanut butter. Quickly add carob powder and then all the seeds, coconut, and fruit. Pour into square pan and refrigerate to harden. Cut into squares. Keep in the refrigerator if possible.

Natural Health Candy

½ pound dates
1 pound dried figs
2 cups chopped walnuts
½ cup seedless raisins

1 pound dried apricots
1 teaspoon grated orange rind,
    sesame seeds, or shredded,
    unsweetened coconut

Put all ingredients, except rind, seeds, or coconut, through food grinder. Mix well. Press into buttered dish and cut into squares. Roll in rind, seeds, or coconut.

EQUIVALENTS, NOTES, INDEX

Equivalents

a pinch or a dash	=	slightly less than ⅛ teaspoon
3 teaspoons	=	1 tablespoon
4 tablespoons	=	¼ cup
5 tablespoons	=	⅓ cup less 1 tablespoon
8 tablespoons	=	½ cup
12 tablespoons	=	¾ cup
16 tablespoons	=	1 cup
2 tablespoons	=	1 liquid ounce
1 cup	=	½ pint
4 cups flour	=	1 pound
2 cups liquid	=	16 fluid ounces
4 cups liquid	=	1 quart
⅔ cup honey	=	1 cup sugar (in sweetness)
5 large eggs	=	1 cup
8 egg whites	=	1 cup
12–15 egg yolks	=	1 cup
¼ pound (stick) butter	=	½ cup
1 cup butter	=	½ pound
2 cups grated cheese	=	½ pound
1 cup uncooked rice	=	2 cups cooked
1 cup uncooked macaroni	=	2 cups cooked
1 cup uncooked noodles	=	1¼ cups cooked
¼ cup lemon juice	=	1 lemon
1¼ cups prunes or raisins	=	½ pound
1½ pounds apples	=	1 quart
1 cup chopped nuts	=	5 ounces

Notes

An electric yogurt maker may be obtained from

International Yogurt Company
628 North Doheny Drive
Los Angeles, California 90069

A complete list of organic food sources in the United States is: *Guide to Organic Food Shopping and Organic Living*, Editorial Staff of Rodale Press (Rodale Press, 33 East Minor Street, Emmaus, Pennsylvania 18049), $1.00.

Other books we recommend on the preparation of natural foods are:

Adelle Davis, *Let's Cook It Right*, revised edition (New York: Signet Books, New American Library, 1970), $1.50.
Ellen and Vrest Orton, *Cooking with Whole Grain* (New York: Farrar, Straus & Giroux, Inc., 1951), $1.95.
Beatrice Trum Hunter, *The Natural Foods Cookbook* (New York: Simon and Schuster, 1969), $2.95.

Index